WALKING CINCINNATI

52 Scenic Hikes Through
Our Parks and Neighborhoods

by Darcy & Robert Folzenlogen

WILLOW PRESS
Glendale, Ohio

D1218426

ISBN: 0-9620685-1-9
Library of Congress Catalog Card Number 89-50227

Published by Willow Press, Glendale, Ohio
Printed by Otto Zimmerman & Son Company, Inc.,
   Newport, Kentucky
Typesetting by Blue Chip Composition,
   Silverton, Ohio

For Sarah and Zach

ACKNOWLEDGEMENTS

Our sincere thanks to the many librarians, clerks, principals, secretaries and public relations personnel whose insight and assistance were instrumental in the production of this guide. Special thanks to the following persons for their generous contribution to our research:

Ms. Cindy Abell, Hughes High School
Mr. Charles Carey, Xavier University
Ms. Mildred Hargreaves, Cincinnati Park Board
Ms. Anne Keller, Public Library of Cincinnati & Hamilton County
Mr. Steve Kottsy, Milford Historical Society
Ms. Sabrina Nelson, Pleasant Ridge
Ms. Mary O'Driscoll, Montgomery Historical Society
Mr. Ellis Rawnsley, Terrace Park
Ms. Vivian Wagner, Cincinnati Park Board
Ms. Claire Young, University of Cincinnati
Mr. Ken Ziegel, Hyde Park Community United Methodist Church

We also wish to thank the staffs at Blue Chip Composition and Otto Zimmerman & Son Printing Company for their diligence, patience and technical assistance.

Finally, to Sarah and Zach......thanks for your company, your good humor and your perseverance.

Contents

FOREWORD

Two hundred years after her first citizens camped across from the Licking River, Cincinnati has grown into a vibrant metropolitan area with a population approaching 1.5 million. The city's economic health is matched by her cultural diversity and the regional topography has favored the development of distinct neighborhoods.

To the benefit of today's residents, Cincinnati's forefathers ensured that open space would be conserved by establishing a superb network of municipal and county parks. In addition, attention to our city's heritage has resulted in the preservation and renovation of many historic buildings and monuments.

This guide offers 52 walking tours through some of Cincinnati's most scenic and historic areas. We have included urban, suburban and natural settings in an effort to emphasize the city's diversity. Each walk is illustrated with a map and a photo to depict the layout and character of that area. Trail mileage, local terrain and directions for reaching each area are provided.

We hope that this guide will encourage Tristate residents and visitors to leave their cars and explore Cincinnati's parks and neighborhoods on foot. They will certainly benefit from the exercise and, hopefully, will gain a better appreciation for our city's political, cultural and natural heritage. Perhaps then the future protection of these resources will be assured.

Darcy and Robert Folzenlogen

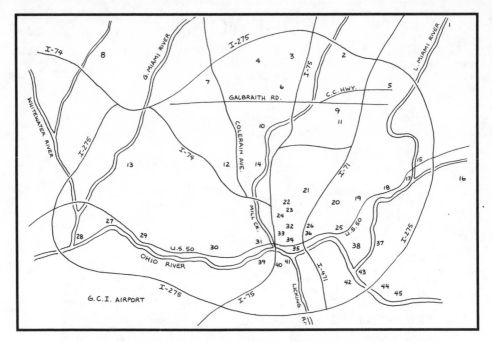

LOCATION OF HIKING AREAS

1. Little Miami Scenic Trail
2. Sharon Woods
3. Glendale
4. Winton Woods
5. Old Montgomery
6. Wyoming
7. Farbach-Werner N.P.
8. Miami Whitewater Forest
9. French Park
10. Caldwell Park
11. Pleasant Ridge
12. Mt. Airy Forest
13. Mitchell Memorial Forest
14. Spring Grove Cemetery
15. Milford
16. Cincinnati Nature Center
17. Terrace Park
18. Mariemont
19. Ault Park/Observatory Historic District
20. Hyde Park
21. Xavier University/Avondale
22. Clifton
23. University of Cincinnati
24. Fairview Park
25. Alms Park/Mt. Lookout
26. Eden Park
27. Harrison Memorial/ Congress Green
28. Shawnee Lookout Park
29. Sayler Park
30. Embshoff Woods & N.P.
31. Mt. Echo Park
32. Over-the-Rhine/Liberty Hill
33. Plum St./Central Parkway/ Eighth St.
34. Skywalk/Fountain Square/ Fifth St.
35. Cincinnati Riverfront/Lytle Park Historic District
36. Mt. Adams
37. Stanbery Park
38. Lunken Airport
39. Devou Park
40. West Covington/MainStrasse
41. Covington Riverfront District/ Suspension Bridge
42. Fort Thomas Military Reservation/ Tower Park
43. California Woods
44. Withrow Nature Preserve
45. Woodland Mound Park

TRAIL DATA

Hike	Mileage	Terrain
1. Little Miami Scenic Trail	Variable	flat
2. Sharon Woods		
Gorge Trail	1.25	hilly; steep areas
Hike/Bike Trail	3.0	flat
3. Glendale	2.6	rolling
4. Winton Woods		
Hike/Bike Trail	2.8	flat
Kingfisher Trail	1.1	rolling; few steep areas
5. Old Montgomery	2.0	flat
6. Wyoming	2.6	flat
7. Farbach-Werner N.P.		
Pin Oak Trail	.9	flat
8. Miami Whitewater Forest		
Badlands Trail	1.75	hilly; steep areas
9. French Park	1.3	rolling; few steep areas
10. Caldwell Park	1.4	hilly; steep areas
11. Pleasant Ridge	2.2	rolling; long hill
12. Mt. Airy Forest	4.0	hilly; steep areas
13. Mitchell Memorial Forest		
Wood Duck Trail	1.3	flat
14. Spring Grove Cemetery	3.8	rolling
15. Milford	2.4	rolling
16. Cincinnati Nature Center		
Powel Crosley Lake Trail	.8	mostly flat; few hills
Lookout Trail	2.0	rolling; few hills
17. Terrace Park	3.2	flat
18. Mariemont	2.4	flat
19. Ault Park/Observatory		
Historic District	3.0	rolling
20. Hyde Park	2.8	rolling
21. Xavier University/Avondale	2.0	hilly; few steep areas
22. Clifton	5.2	rolling
23. University of Cincinnati	2.0	rolling
24. Fairview Park	1.7	hilly; steep areas
25. Alms Park/Mt. Lookout	4.6	hilly; few steep areas
26. Eden Park	2.8	rolling; few steep areas
27. Harrison Memorial/Congress		
Green	.5	gentle hill; few steps
28. Shawnee Lookout Park		
Miami Fort Trail	1.5	hilly; few steep areas
Little Turtle Trail	2.0	hilly; few steep areas
Blue Jacket Trail	1.3	hilly; few steep areas

29. Sayler Park	3.0	mostly flat; few hills
30. Embshoff Woods & N.P.		
Parcours Trail	1.0	rolling
31. Mt. Echo Park	1.25	rolling
32. Over-the-Rhine/Liberty Hill	1.2	hilly; steep areas
33. Plum St./Central Parkway/		
Eighth St.	1.8	flat
34. Skywalk/Fountain Square/		
Fifth St.	1.8	flat; few stairways
35. Cincinnati Riverfront/Lytle		
Park Historic District	2.6	mostly flat; stairways
36. Mt. Adams	1.4	hilly; steep areas
37. Stanbery Park		
Stanbery Creek Trail	1.5	hilly; steep areas
38. Lunken Airport		
Hike/Bike Trail	6.2	flat
39. Devou Park		
Nature Trail	1.25	hilly; steep areas
Overlook Hike	2.2	rolling
40. West Covington/		
MainStrasse	2.7	flat
41. Covington Riverside		
District/Suspension Bridge	2.5	mostly flat; stairways
42. Fort Thomas Military		
Reservation/Tower Park	1.4	flat
43. California Woods		
California Junction Trail	1.25	hilly; few steep areas
Combined Trail	2.0	hilly; few steep areas
44. Withrow Nature Preserve		
Trout Lily Trail	2.0	
Old Farm Loop		rolling
Hepatica Hill Loop		steep hills
45. Woodland Mound Park		
Combined Trail	1.8	hilly; steep areas

KEY TO MAPS

Roads:

Parking Areas:

Trails:

Lakes/Streams:

Forest/Woodlands:

Marsh:

Building/Structure:

Stairways:

Railroad:

Bridges:

1 LITTLE MIAMI SCENIC TRAIL

Distance: variable
Terrain: flat

The headwaters of the Little Miami River lie in west-central Ohio, just east of Springfield. The stream winds southwestward, cutting a narrow gorge west of Clifton before crossing the farmlands of Greene County. In Warren County it flows through a deep valley which gradually widens as the stream enters the southern counties of Ohio.

Designated a National Scenic River, the Little Miami is a mecca for canoeists, fishermen and naturalists. With the opening of the Little Miami Scenic Trail access to hikers and cyclists has been greatly improved.

A paved, 13-mile section of the trail parallels the river from Loveland to Morrow, Ohio. It follows the route of the old Little Miami Railroad which first chugged through the valley in the 1840's.

Mileage markers along the way document your progress and your hike can be limited to whatever distance you desire. Wooden bridges cross the side streams and river overlooks are spaced along the route. Much of the scenery is "closed-in" by trees in the summer and views are more expansive during the colder months. For those starting in Loveland, a popular destination is Foster, Ohio, approximately 3.5 miles upstream. The Montgomery Rd. bridge arches high above the river just south of Foster.

To reach the Loveland trailhead from Cincinnati, follow I-71 North and then I-275 East. Take the Loveland-Indian Hill Exit (Exit #52). Turn left (north) and drive 3 miles into Loveland. Turn right on Loveland Ave., cross the bridge and turn left at the second street (Railroad Ave.). Free parking is provided.

If possible, plan to visit on a weekday. Throngs of cyclists congest the area on weekends, especially during the warmer months. The paved route discussed above is actually the middle section of a longer, earthen trail, extending from Kroger Hills Park, near Terrace Park, to the Spring Valley Wildlife Area north of Waynesville, Ohio. The complete route totals 44 miles; plans are underway to pave the 8.5 mile section between Loveland and Milford.

6

Scene along the Little Miami

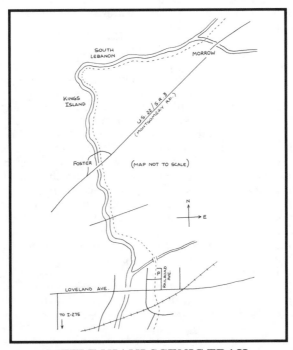

LITTLE MIAMI SCENIC TRAIL

7

2 SHARON WOODS

Gorge Trail
    Distance: 1.25 miles
    Terrain: hilly; steep areas

Hike/Bike Trail
    Distance: 3.0 miles
    Terrain: flat

Established in 1932, Sharon Woods is the oldest of Hamilton County's Parks. Its 737 acres of forest and meadow, centered around a 35 acre lake, provide recreation for thousands of visitors each year. In addition, the historic Sharon Woods Village, a collection of restored 19th Century buildings, offers a taste of Cincinnati's rural past.

To reach the Park, take I-75 to I-275. Follow I-275 east and take the Mason-Sharonville Exit (Exit #46). Turn right (south) on Route 42 and drive approximately 1 mile to the Park entrance. Daily usage fee is $1.00 per vehicle or you can purchase an annual pass to all Hamilton County Parks for $3.00.

Sharon Woods contains two excellent hiking trails as illustrated on the map.

Gorge Trail. This 1.25 mile trail loops through a beautiful woodland flanking the course of Sharon Creek. The stream has cut a deep ravine through the ancient bedrock, exposing cliffs of shale and limestone. Fossil hunters will find numerous bryozoans and brachiopods in these Ordovician sea deposits. The forest's abundant wildlife includes pileated woodpeckers, barred owls and flying squirrels.

Park in the small lot just east of the dam (see map). Walk back across the dam and enter the trail on the west side of Sharon Creek. The trail roller-coasters along the gorge wall before angling sharply to the right and ascending the

ridge via a wide switchback. At the top, an overlook yields a stunning view of Sharon Creek as it snakes through the gorge.

After a short course along the ridge, the trail descends into the gorge via a series of wooden stairs. Turn left at the trail intersection, crossing the bridge that spans Sharon Creek. Continuing northward the path skirts the Park's golf course and gradually ascends along the eastern flank of the gorge. Halfway along this section an overlook provides a view of one of the stream's many small waterfalls.

Hike/Bike Trail. This paved, 3 mile trail winds around Sharon Lake, alternately hugging the shoreline or cutting through adjacent woodlands. A good starting point is at the Park's Marina, just off Kemper Rd., where ample parking is available.

Descend from the Marina's lot, turn left and follow the trail as it parallels the shore. Pass under Kemper Rd. and continue northward. Restoration of the lake, accomplished over the past two years, has greatly altered the backwater ecosystem. Prior to the onslaught of bulldozers, an extensive marshland fanned out from the north inlets, spreading along the shallow lake margins. This wetland harbored waterfowl, herons and other aquatic creatures. Hopefully, some recovery of the marsh will occur after nature is left alone.

The Gorge Trail

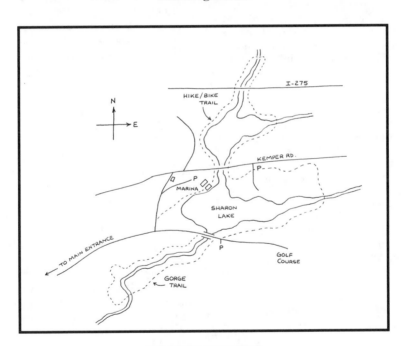

SHARON WOODS

Crossing under I-275, the visitor encounters other, more vivid examples of man's impact on nature. Graffiti, litter, fumes and road noise detract from the beauty and serenity of this wild oasis.

The trail loops across the lake's north inlet and turns southward, winding along the shore and crossing another feeder stream. After passing under Kemper Rd. the trail angles to the left, bisects a small woodland and leads into a parking lot. Cross the lot and pick up the trail as it winds through an area of thickets and immature forest.

Descending into the east inlet ravine, the trail crosses the stream, ascends along the golf course and emerges onto the road. Continue westward, crossing the dam, and turn right at the intersection for a short walk back to the Marina.

3 GLENDALE

Distance: 2.6 miles
Terrain: rolling

Glendale, Ohio, the oldest planned subdivision in our State, was initially platted by Robert C. Phillips in 1851. Six hundred acres of wooded hillside had been purchased by the Glendale Association as a residential retreat for some of Cincinnati's early industrialists. Located along the newly completed Cincinnati-Hamilton-Dayton Railroad, the village was easily accessible from the city's industrial corridor.

Incorporated in 1855, Glendale has retained its small-town, New England flavor. It's winding, gas-lit streets are lined with large, Victorian homes. Tall oak trees shade the generous lawns and small parks are spaced through the village. The Glendale Historic District, encompassing 392 acres, was added to the National Register of Historic Places in July, 1976.

To reach Glendale, follow I-75 to the Sharonville-Glendale Exit (Exit #15). Turn west on Sharon Rd. and drive 1 mile into the village. Just across the railroad tracks, turn left into the Village Square. Park here or along one of the avenues leading into the square.

Dating from Glendale's inception, the Railroad Depot (1) has since served as a community center, council chambers, jail and potting shop. Its use is now limited to railroad storage and maintenance. The Iron Horse Inn (2) occupies the former home of the Bracker Tavern, which opened in the mid 1800's.

Walk west along Fountain Ave. The small park at the intersection with Woodbine Ave. is named for William VanCleve, who willed his estate to the village for maintenance of its open spaces. Just southeast of the park is the First Presbyterian Church (3). The small, buttressed structure, completed in 1860, was Glendale's first church. The larger church was added in 1873.

Continue westward on Fountain Ave. The John R. Wright House (4), at Fountain & Laurel, dates from 1855. The brickwork around its arched, Florentine windows is especially attractive. The one-story frame house at 95 Fountain Ave. (5) is the former home of Charles Sawyer, Ohio Lieutenant Governor and President Truman's Secretary of Commerce.

Cross through Floral Park (6) which was set aside as open space in 1851. At the top of the ridge is the Robert's House (7), a Classic-Revival structure dating from 1855. It reportedly served as a hiding place for slaves during the Civil War.

Continue along Fountain and turn right on Congress Ave. The Gothic, frame Swedenborgian Church (8) was built in 1861. Just north of the Church is the Glendale Lyceum (9), a social and recreational center since 1891.

The tile-roofed Glendale Elementary School (10), dating from the late 1800's, underwent extensive reconstruction in 1901. Across Erie Ave. from the school is the McLean-Johnston House (11). Built in 1855, this large, brick home was formerly a hotel and a boys school during its long career.

On the southeast corner of Congress Ave. and Sharon Rd. is The Grand Finale (12), known throughout the Tristate. The restaurant, which opened in 1975, is especially renowned for its desserts and Sunday brunch. Looking west along Sharon Rd. you will see the church and school of St. Gabriel's Parish (13). Organized in 1858, the parish's stone, Romanesque church was dedicated in 1907.

Turn right (east) on Sharon Rd. The Town Hall and Village Firehouse (14) date from 1875. Across Sharon Rd. from the Hall is Glendale's War Memorial (15), backed by a stone, cylindrical structure (16). The latter is a remnant of Glendale's first water tower. Built in 1892, the upper tower collapsed thirty years later.

The Episcopal Church (17) on Forest Ave. was dedicated in 1868. One of its architects was Samuel Hannaford who also designed Cincinnati's Music Hall. Walk south on Forest Ave. which winds back to Floral Park. Cut across the park and continue south along Ivy Ave. The Robbins house (18), at 780 Ivy Ave., offers

Glendale's Village Square

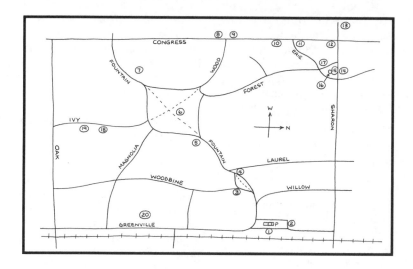

GLENDALE

a fine example of French Renaissance Revival architecture, including a mansard roof. The large, brick house at 740 Ivy (19) is the former home of Warner M. Bateman, U.S. District Attorney for President Grant.

Turn left and descend along Oak St. A wide greenbelt, preserved along Glendale's southern border, buffers the village from nearby industrial plants.

Turn left along Greenville Ave. which parallels the railroad tracks. Many of the small, frame houses along this street were built in the 1850's, providing homes for the laborers who worked on the C.H. & D. Railroad. Contrasting with these small homes are the grand estates of the Railroad executives. The former home of Daniel McLaren, Superintendent of the Railroad, sits far from the tracks at 815 Greenville Ave. (20).

Returning to the Village Square, your tour of Glendale has totalled 2.6 miles.

4 WINTON WOODS

Hike/Bike Trail
  Distance: 2.8 miles
  Terrain: flat
Kingfisher Trail
  Distance: 1.1 mile
  Terrain: rolling; few steep areas

Winton Woods is both the second oldest and the second largest member of the Hamilton County Park District. Established in 1939, the Park now encompasses 2133 acres of forest, field and water surface. Its 188 acre lake and adjacent picnic grounds attract the majority of the annual visitors.

Winton Woods offers several hiking trails, two of which are discussed below.

Hike/Bike Trail. Winton Woods' paved Hike/Bike trail offers an appealing and a convenient avenue for exercise. Park in one of the lots .7 mile west of Winton Rd. (see map). Follow the path as it loops westward and then eastward, straddling the shoreline of West Fork Lake. Bird enthusiasts will find that these shallow backwaters attract a variety of ducks, herons and shorebirds.

Wind eastward, eventually crossing under Winton Rd. The trail loops to the north, skirting an arm of the lake. It then circles around the Park's central recreation area before branching to the east and west along Lakeview Drive.

Turn left (west) paralleling the drive and crossing over Winton Rd. Continue .7 mile to the parking lot. Your walk has totalled 2.8 miles.

Kingfisher Trail. For those interested in a shorter hike (or as an addition to the longer walk), we suggest the Kingfisher Trail. This 1.1 mile loop starts just north and west of the parking lots, as illustrated on the map. Enter the forest for a short distance and turn left, descending a short set of stairs to the level of the Kingfisher wetland. Boardwalks elevate the trail as it skirts the soggy ground and offer viewpoints from which visitors can peruse the marsh. Watch for herons, ducks and an occasional rail. If you're lucky you may spot a mink as it hunts along the bank. The wetland is named for the belted kingfishers that noisily patrol the area.

The trail leads northward, following a tributary of West Fork Creek. After winding upstream for 1/3 mile, the trail angles to the right, climbing into the forest. It then curves southward, meandering through the woods before merging with the entry trail. Educational plaques, spaced along the route, illustrate some of nature's handiwork that can be found in this transitional habitat.

To reach Winton Woods from Cincinnati, take I-75 north and then I-275 west, toward Indianapolis. Drive approximately 4 miles and take the Forest Park/Greenhills Exit (Exit #39). Follow Winton Rd. south for 3 miles to the Park entrance. Turn right and proceed .7 mile to the parking lots. The daily usage fee is currently $1.00 per vehicle (or an annual pass to all Hamilton County Parks can be obtained for $3.00).

The Kingfisher Wetland

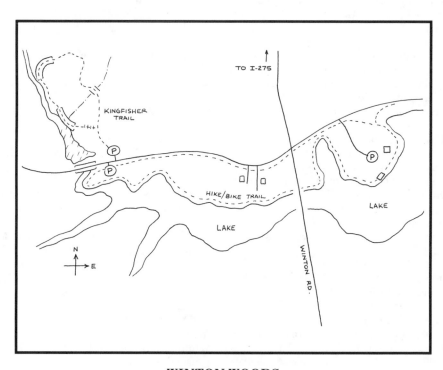

WINTON WOODS

5 OLD MONTGOMERY

Distance: 2.0 miles
Terrain: flat

Montgomery, Ohio, was first settled in 1795 when six families arrived in the area from Orange County, New York. Among these pioneers was Nathaniel Terwilliger who officially planned the village in 1802. Incorporated in 1910, Montgomery gained "city" status in 1971.

During the past two decades Montgomery has experienced phenomenal growth and residential zones have exploded across its theretofore rural calm. In an effort to preserve its historic structures and pioneer heritage, city officials have promoted a restoration of "Old Montgomery" and have ensured that new buildings blend with its 19th Century flavor.

For a 2-mile walking tour of Old Montgomery, park in the lot at Swaim Park, which is bordered by Cooper and Zig Zag Roads. The Park is a remnant of Swaim Field, a golf course that succumbed to Montgomery's population explosion.

Follow the walkway to Zig Zag Rd. and turn right. The frame house on the northwest corner of Cooper and Zig Zag dates from 1832. Known as the Wilder/Swaim Farm House (1), it was built by James and Susan Wilder who moved to the area from Rhode Island. It is now home to the Montgomery Historical Society.

Turn left (east) along Cooper Rd. The home at 7786 Cooper (2) dates from 1830, having been built by Montgomery's first postmaster, Joseph Taulman. The small building (3) at Cooper and Shelly Ln. was Montgomery's first civic building, serving as town hall and jail from 1925 to 1969.

Turn left along Montgomery Rd. One of Cincinnati's main arteries, this road follows the route of an early stagecoach line. Many of Montgomery's most popular shops and restaurants line its walkways, some occupying structures that have graced the avenue for over 150 years. The Universalist Church (4) dates from 1837 and is included in the National Register of Historic Places.

Turn right along Remington Rd., walk 1 block and turn right on Main St. The Jonathan Crain House (5), at 9441 Main, was built in 1845. Both Cooper Rd. and Main St. follow the route of old Indian trails. The "Yost Tavern" (6), on the northwest corner of these streets, has occupied the site since 1809.

Turn left on Cooper Rd. and walk 1 block to the Indian Hill line. Cross the street and backtrack along Cooper. The Victorian "Choate House" (7), at 7967 Cooper, dates from 1890 while the "Patmore/Lumley House" (8), at 7919 Cooper was built in 1810.

Walk north on Montgomery Rd. and turn left along Remington. The "Smethurst House" (9), on the northwest corner of Montgomery and Remington, was built in 1865 for the local shoemaker. The "Blair/Barker House" (10), at 7844 Remington, dates from 1875. Continue west on Remington to Zig Zag Road. Turn left and walk back to Swaim Park.

To reach Montgomery take I-71 and Exit onto the Cross County Highway (Exit #14). Drive east and the highway will soon end at Montgomery Rd. Follow Montgomery Rd. north into the central village area, turn left on Cooper Rd. and proceed to Swaim Park.

Scene along Montgomery Rd.

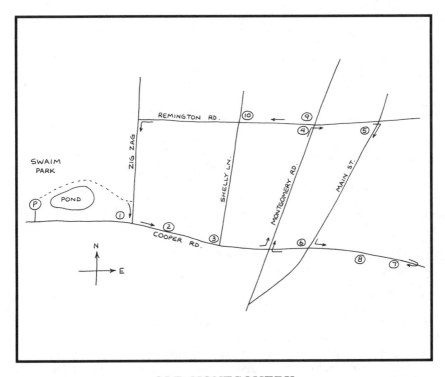

OLD MONTGOMERY

6 WYOMING

Distance: 2.6 miles
Terrain: flat

The area that is now Wyoming, Ohio, was first settled around 1800. The village itself was founded by Robert Reily in 1861 and was named after a valley in northeastern Pennsylvania. Centered at the junction of three large farms (the Burns, Wilmuth and Riddle estates), Wyoming was first platted in 1869 and was eventually incorporated in 1874.

For a walking tour of this attractive neighborhood, park at the community pool and recreation area (1) on Springfield Pike (see map). Walk south along Springfield Pike, the northern extension of Vine St. At the corner of Wyoming Ave. and Springfield Pike a plaque (2) commemorates the founding of the village by Robert Reily. Across from this intersection, at 507 Springfield Pike (3), is the former home of the Riddle family, built in 1835.

Walk east along Wyoming Ave. The Wyoming Middle School (4) occupies the south-central portion of the block. Just east of the school, at 129 Wyoming Ave. (5), is the Stearns/Compton House, built by the founder of the Stearns & Foster Mattress Company, in Lockland. Across the street, at 132 Wyoming Ave. (6), is the John Wilmuth Hill House, built in 1870. The attractive house at 212 Wyoming (7) dates from the 1890's and provides an excellent example of Queen Anne architecture. On your right, at 217 Wyoming Ave. (8), is a wooden, Gothic style house that served as a parsonage for over 100 years.

The Presbyterian Church (9), at Burns and Wyoming Avenues, was built in 1890. This beautiful, Romanesque Revival structure was designed by Samuel Hannaford who also designed Cincinnati's Music Hall.

Turn right (south) along Burns Ave. and then right on Worthington. The first three houses on your right (10) are "sister houses," all of frame construction and initially identical in floor plan. They date from the 1860's. Farther along, the house at 200 Worthington (11), completed after the Civil War, affords a fine example of Italianate architectural style.

Angle to the left along Beech Ave., then left on Walnut St. and finally left on Elm Ave. At the intersection of Elm and Burns Avenues, look to the south for a view of Wyoming Baptist Church (12). This white frame building, topped by an attractive gray and red, shingled steeple, was completed in 1882.

Walk north along Burns Ave. The house at 233 Burns (13) dates from 1865. From the corner of Burns and S. Cooper, one can see the white-pillared, Italianate Gideon-Palmer House (14). Perched on a hillock, this striking home was built in the 1860's and remained in the same family through four generations.

Turn right (east) on S. Cooper and then left along Grove Ave. The 300 block of Grove (15) is characterized by colorful, frame, Victorian houses. All date from the 1890's and were built as twins or triplicates. The block seems to be an early, more appealing predecessor of our modern, repetitive subdivisions.

Proceed north along Grove Ave., turn left on Wyoming Ave. and then right on Burns. Walk 1 block and turn left on Wilmuth. This handsome block is characterized by a blend of Victorian and Tudor homes, all blessed with spacious, shaded lots.

Turn right (north) along Springfield Pike and return to the community park. Your walking tour of Wyoming has totalled 2.6 miles.

To reach Wyoming, take I-75 to the Galbraith Rd. Exit (Exit # 10-B). Drive west on Galbraith for a few blocks and turn right on Vine St., which becomes Springfield Pike. The community park will be approximately 1.7 miles on your right.

The Gideon - Palmer House

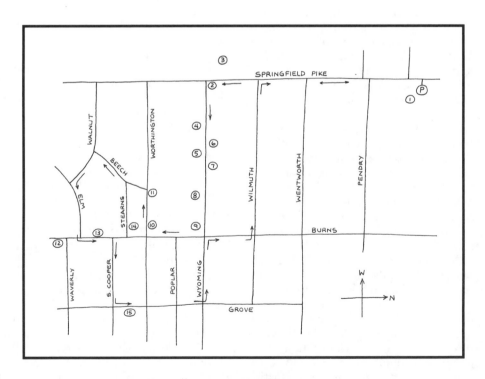

WYOMING

7 FARBACH-WERNER NATURE PRESERVE

Pin Oak Trail
  Distance: .9 mile
  Terrain: flat

Most nature preserves are large tracts of abandoned or "unusable" land on the outskirts of metropolitan areas. Management often involves little more than restricting access and letting nature take its course.

More challenging is the protection and maintenance of small preserves in heavily developed areas. There, habitat destruction is continually threatened by political, economic and commercial forces. Farbach-Werner Nature Preserve, in the northwest suburbs of Cincinnati, is such a place.

Donated to the Hamilton County Park District by Elizabeth and Alfred Werner, the preserve was added to the Park system in 1972. Its 23 acres of field and woodland are bounded on three sides by a bustling residential and commercial zone. To the west, a small farm buffers the preserve from additional human pressure.

Farbach-Werner is a popular site for seasonal festivals and nature programs throughout the year. An educational barn (1) and a nature-oriented gift shop (Nature's Niche, 2) are on the premises.

The .9 mile **Pin Oak Trail** winds through the refuge. Connecting trails permit a variable route and add to the potential length of your hike. Starting near the barn, the trail first skirts a small pond where turtles, frogs and tadpoles are easily found during the warmer months. It then loops through an open woodland before entering a small tract of forest. A 'drum nest" (3) near the west end of these woods has been used by a pair of great horned owls; look for them in February and March.

Beyond the forest the trail follows the border of the preserve's central meadow, where wildflowers are abundant in late summer. American woodcocks use this field for their famous mating flights in early spring.

The Park District provides a trail-guide brochure that points out many of the area's natural highlights. Brochures are usually available outside the gift shop or at the trailhead. Plan to visit during each season to witness the changes of flora and fauna that characterize nature's cycle.

To reach Farbach-Werner Nature Preserve, take I-75 north and then I-275 west toward Indianapolis. Exit onto Colerain Ave. (U.S. 27) and turn left (south). Drive approximately 1.5 miles and turn right on Poole Rd. The entrance will be 1 block on your left. A daily usage fee of $1.00 per vehicle is charged; an annual pass to all Hamilton County Parks can be obtained for $3.00.

The Pin Oak Trail

FARBACH-WERNER NATURE PRESERVE

8   MIAMI WHITEWATER FOREST

Badlands Trail
  Distance: 1.75 miles
  Terrain: hilly; steep areas

With 2359 acres of forest, meadows and lake surface, Miami Whitewater is the largest of Hamilton County's Parks. This extensive preserve sprawls across a wooded ridge, approximately 15 miles west of Cincinnati. The daily usage fee is $1.00 per vehicle or an annual pass to all County Parks can be obtained for $3.00.

To reach the Park, follow I-74 west toward Indiana. Exit on Dry Fork Rd. (Exit #3). Turn right (north) and drive 1 mile to West Rd. Turn right, cross Dry Fork Creek and turn left along the Park's entry road. Past the toll booth (1) follow the road as it curves to the right. At the stop sign continue straight ahead and up the hill to the Bird Museum parking lot (see map).

Miami Whitewater Forest is a popular place for picnics, fishing, birdwatching and hiking. While there are several excellent trails in the Park, we recommend the **Badlands Trail** which winds through some of the Forest's most interesting topography. The trailhead is just west of the Bird Museum (2).

This 1.75 mile trail loops through a parcel of forest that is cut by numerous ravines. As a result, the route is hilly and several steep sections occur along the way. In particular, some of the stream banks can present a challenge after heavy spring rains. However, the trail is easily followed and footing is good throughout most of the hike.

A trail brochure, available at the Park's ranger station, highlights some of the

birds, animals and plants that inhabit the forest. The predominant beech-maple-oak woodland is dotted with small stands of cedar, tulip and black cherry trees. Wildflowers, Christmas ferns, honeysuckle and wild grapes are easily found in season. The forest's abundant birdlife includes pileated woodpeckers, Cooper's hawks and barred owls. Yellow-billed cuckoos, ruby-throated hummingbirds and hooded warblers are among the summer residents. Local mammals include white-tailed deer, woodchucks, raccoons, striped skunks, chipmunks and flying squirrels. Watch for their tracks in the mud or snow.

Enter the forest, walk a short distance and bear left where the path forks. Heading southwest, the trail winds along a ridge before turning northward. Gradually ascending toward the woodland's highest ground, the route crosses several small streams.

At the northern end of the loop the trail enters an area where stream erosion has cut a network of small ridges and shallow ravines. These earthen formations offer a miniature replica of South Dakota's "Badlands," where water has carved countless peaks and valleys through the soft bedrock of sandstone and shale.

After snaking eastward through these "badlands," the trail turns to the south, descending into a deep ravine and then climbing onto the next ridge. This pattern is repeated for two more stream crossings before the path merges with the entry trail.

Winter in "The Badlands"

**THE BADLANDS
TRAIL**

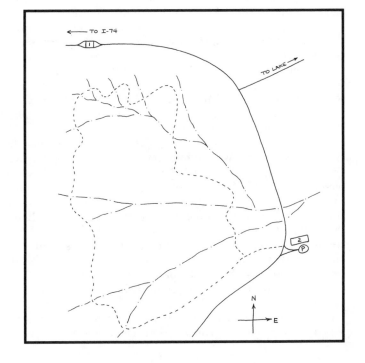

9 FRENCH PARK

Distance: 1.3 miles
Terrain: rolling; few steep areas

French Park, in Amberley Village, is a popular spot for family picnics in the summer, kite flying in the fall, and sled riding in the winter. Its 276 acres spread across a gentle slope, half covered by open lawns and half by a beautiful, hardwood forest.

The area was donated to the city of Cincinnati by the late Herbert G. French, whose vast estate was known as Reachmont Farm. The French house (5) still sits on the property, its second floor utilized as office space by several conservation groups.

To reach the Park, take I-71 to the Ridge Rd. North Exit (Exit #8-B). Follow Ridge Rd. north for approximately 2 miles. Turn right (east) on Section Rd. and watch for the Park entrance on your left.

Park in one of the lots near this entrance (see map). Walk along the road, cross the bridge and bear left across a picnic/play area. The trail starts across the creek (see map), heading northeast. It first bisects a secluded picnic area and then enters the forest, winding along the stream. After walking approximately 50 yds. through the woods, watch for a spur trail that crosses the creek for a short distance before re-joining the main trail upstream.

Once past this alternate loop watch for a small grave marker (1) on your left. The weathered plaque pays tribute to Sammy, Nick, Pete, Pal and Robert, "faithful friends" of Reachmont Farm.

Continue eastward along the north side of the stream. Birdwatching can be excellent here and fossil buffs will enjoy perusing the Ordovician rocks that jut from the steep creek bed. Numerous small waterfalls interrupt the stream and its tributaries, their muffled gurgling adding to the peacefulness of this woodland.

Near the top of the ravine the trail splits into three routes (see map). Cross the creek and climb through the forest, emerging across from the hilltop shelter house (2). From this open ridge the visitor has a broad view of the Mill Creek Valley to the west, backed by the high ground of Mt. Airy and Finneytown. Sunsets can be spectacular from here.

Descend along the Park's central drive. Halfway down is a cluster of buildings...a service barn (3), the caretaker's home (4), and the French House (5). The latter has fallen into disrepair but renovations are hopefully planned in the near future. Rivers Unlimited, Hillside Trust and Little Miami Inc. have offices on the second floor.

Continue down the road to your car, completing a 1.3 mile loop. We recommend a winter visit, free from the noise and crowds of summer.

Broad Lawns of the French Estate

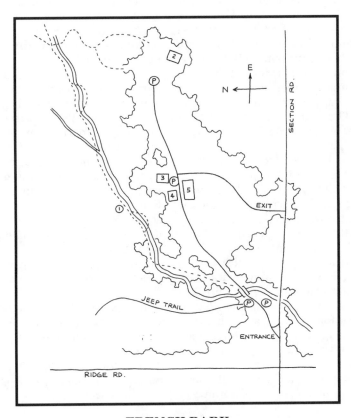

FRENCH PARK

10 CALDWELL PARK

Distance: 1.4 miles (variable)
Terrain: hilly; steep areas

Draped over a series of ridges and ravines, Caldwell Park's forest preserve covers 133 acres, flanking the west bank of the Mill Creek. Access to this beech-maple woodland is via a network of trails, maintained by the Cincinnati Park Board The primary route, dedicated in July, 1976, is named for Ray Abercrombie, the first scoutmaster of Boy Scout Troop 14.

This little known and sparsely utilized preserve was actually set aside as park land back in 1914, a donation from the descendants of Major James Caldwell. During its early years, much of the park was utilized as a nursery and orchard, supplying plant seedlings for other Cincinnati parks.

To reach the preserve, follow I-75 to the Paddock Rd./Seymour Ave. Exit (Exit #9). Turn west on Paddock Rd. Just beyond the underpass, angle left on North Bend Rd. Drive approximately 1 mile to the forest preserve parking lot, on your right. A Nature Center, operated by the Cincinnati Park Board, sits adjacent to the lot. The center is utilized for educational programs but is not regularly open to the public.

Follow the Abercrombie Trail (1) which begins just north of the parking area. Walk about 100 yards and bear right, descending into the ravine. Cross Ravine Creek and turn left along this trail (2). Wind uphill through a dense woodland and bear right at the intersection. Climb higher into the forest via a stairway.

Emerging onto an abandoned service road, turn right and pick up the Abercrombie Loop Trail (3). Bear left at the fork and follow this trail as it winds along the ridgetop. The mature, open forest permits broad views into the adjacent ravine.

Continue to the east end of the loop where an overlook yields a panorama of the Mill Creek Valley. The view is more expansive in winter when leaves have dropped to the forest floor. Continuing around the end of the loop, watch for a faint trail on your left (4) that leads to another overlook.

Return to the Abercrombie Loop for a short distance and then turn left, descending into the ravine. A log stairway (5) will be noted across the creek. It leads up to the High Bush Loop (6) and Black Locust Trail (7). Of interest is the fact that Ravine Creek disappears beneath the surface above this junction, resurfacing further down the slope where it is fed by natural springs.

Turn right following the Ravine Creek Trail (2) as it winds upstream. Returning to the intersection where you previously climbed to the service road, bear left, cross the creek and ascend a short stairway. Follow this section of the Abercrombie Trail (1) as it loops back to the east, snakes along the ridge and returns to the parking lot. Your hike through the forest has totalled 1.4 miles.

Many of Caldwell Park's trails are partially overgrown during the summer months. To avoid this "closed in" season and to escape the insects and humidity of the mid-summer months, we recommend a visit from October through early May. The numerous maples provide a colorful display in autumn and the hilly terrain is ideal for birding in the spring. Resident mammals include gray squirrels, raccoons, chipmunks, skunk and flying squirrels. The latter are best seen at dusk.

The Park Board's original map of Caldwell Park is now outdated, due to the closure of some trails. We thus suggest that you refer to the map in this book when hiking at the park. As an addition to the route discussed above, you may wish to include the Pawpaw Ridge Loop (8) which leads through mature forest to another overlook. This loop will add .5 mile to your hike.

The Abercrombie Trail

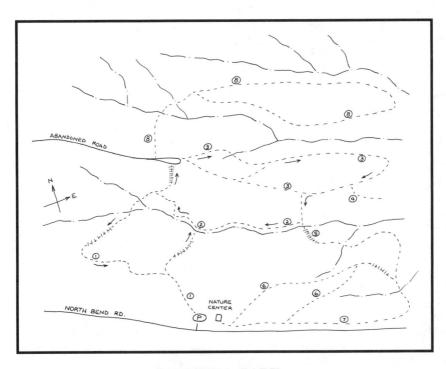

CALDWELL PARK

11   PLEASANT RIDGE

Distance: 2.2 miles
Terrain: rolling; long hill

The territory that is now Pleasant Ridge was first settled in 1795. Col. John McFarland arrived from Pennsylvania and constructed a fort ("McFarland Station") to protect his fellow immigrants from the local Indian tribes. These early settlers were enamored with the area's "pleasant" views, especially those from their ridgetop cemetery. The village thus adopted the name of Pleasant Ridge.

During the early 1800's, the Wood family acquired much of the land in the area and, around 1825, renamed the settlement "Crossroads." This title reflected the town's location at the intersection of a major stagecoach route (now Montgomery Rd.) and a long-established Indian trail (Ridge Rd.). When the area was surveyed for construction of a narrow-gauge railroad, during the mid 1800's, the community was once again referred to as Pleasant Ridge. Finally incorporated in 1891, the village was annexed by Cincinnati in 1912.

While the health of its business district has fluctuated over the years, the neighborhoods of Pleasant Ridge have retained the quiet charm of an earlier era. Indeed, some of the older sections have witnessed a resurgence. For a walking tour through one of the village's more attractive areas, we suggest the following route.

Park along Harvest Ave. near its junction with Ridge Rd. (see map). Walk north along Ridge which was once part of "Columbia Rd." The latter, completed in the 1790's, stretched from Kennedy Heights to Carthage. Across Ridge Rd. are several Victorian homes, each set far from the street and beautifully restored.

Turn right onto Beredith Place which is also lined with renovated homes. This street was renamed during World War II, reportedly during a movement to abolish "German" titles from the village. The current name blends the first names of two sisters, Beryl and Edith, who lived in the neighborhood. Jog to the left as Beredith Place crosses Kincaid Rd. (see map). Continue eastward along Beredith which curves to the right and becomes Parkman Place.

Angle sharply to the left, ascending along Grand Vista Ave. Lined with stately homes and huge shade trees, this street is perhaps the epitome of upscale living. Sitting far from the avenue and well-spaced by broad, manicured lawns, many of these mansion-like homes enjoy a sweeping view of the Mill Creek Valley to the west. At the end of this street, one residence proves that a man's home can be his castle.

Circle back along Grand Vista, Parkman Place and Beredith Place. Turn left on Kincaid Rd. for one block and then right onto Harvest Ave. Returning to your car, your stroll across the Ridge has totalled 2.2 miles.

To reach Pleasant Ridge from other areas of Cincinnati, follow I-71 and take the Ridge Rd. Exit (Exit #8). Drive north on Ridge Rd. for approximately 1 mile, crossing Montgomery Rd. Proceed another ¼ mile and turn right onto Harvest Ave.

Along Grand Vista Avenue

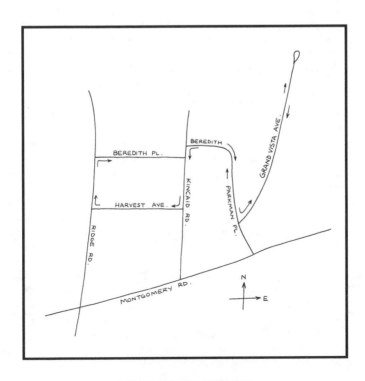

PLEASANT RIDGE

12 MT. AIRY FOREST

Distance: 4.0 miles
Terrain: hilly; steep areas

Mt. Airy Forest, spreading across 1466 acres on Hamilton County's highest ridge, harbors over 10 miles of hiking trails. While the Park's open areas provide numerous picnic sites, its woodlands, resulting from America's largest municipal reforestation project, offer a true back-country experience.

We suggest a trail route that winds for 4 miles through this beautiful forest. Park in the small lot at Picnic Area #21, approximately .9 mile along Trail Ridge Rd. from the Colerain Ave. entrance. Enter the main trail loop via side trails behind the lot (see map).

Turn left along Furnas Trail (A), also called the Overlook Trail, which snakes along the ridge, high above Cedar Ravine. The trail circles Area 22 and then loops through Scotch Pine Ravine. At Area 23, Ponderosa Ridge, the trail emerges into a clearing where a lookout shelter offers a broad view of the I-74 valley.

Re-enter the woods and bear left along Ponderosa Trail (B) which is marked with white slashes; the Quarry Trail (C) splits to the right, descending into White Ash Ravine. The Ponderosa Trail parallels the ridgetop, crossing through a beautiful area of open, mature forest. At the next trail intersection, bear right, crossing a creek.

The trail then snakes through the upper reaches of White Ash Ravine, crossing small tributaries and cutting through a thicket-choked woodland. Bear left at the intersection with Quarry Trail (C) and wind higher along Stone Steps Ridge (Area 19). An area of open, pine forest offers a pleasant respite from the dense, humid woods.

Continue straight ahead through the next trail intersection and descend into Linden Ravine. Here again the mature forest has a pleasing openness, yielding long views into the ravine. Passing Area 18, the trail curves right, crossing Linden Creek via a collapsed bridge. Loop around Hidden Ridge (Area 16) and descend to the Red Oak Ravine.

Ford the stream and turn left, ascending along Red Oak Trail (D), which ends along the Park's Oval. Cross the Oval and pick up the Twin Bridge Trail (E). This unmarked trail is a wide path that starts just to the left of the radio tower (R).

Hike along Sunset Ridge for approximately ¼ mile. Watch for a multi-trail intersection, centered around a sinkhole (X). Turn left and pick up the Furnas Trail (A), marked by blue and white slashes. Loop through the upper reaches of Cedar and Hawthorne Ravines, bearing right where spur trails lead up to Trail Ridge Rd. Passing Area 20, ascend along the ridge wall, cross two small streams and watch for the side trail to Area 21, immediately across from a trail sign. Climb to the parking lot, completing a hike of 4 miles.

To reach Mt. Airy Forest, follow I-75 to I-74 west. Exit onto Colerain Ave. (Exit #18). Turn left (north) on Colerain and drive approximately 1 mile to the Park entrance. Follow Trail Ridge Rd. to Area 21.

The Ponderosa Trail

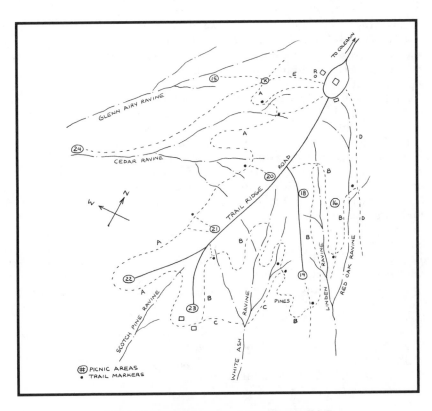

TRAIL RIDGE, MT. AIRY FOREST   29

13 MITCHELL MEMORIAL FOREST

Wood Duck Trail
  Distance: 1.3 miles
  Terrain: flat

Donated to the Hamilton County Park District by William Morris Mitchell, as a memorial to his parents, this 1106 acre preserve is a popular area for picnics. The forest spreads across a ridgetop, just south and east of the Great Miami Valley.

To reach Mitchell Memorial Forest from Cincinnati, follow U.S. 50 (River Rd.) west to Cleves, Ohio. Turn right on Route 264. Drive 3 miles and turn left on Zion Road. After proceeding .8 mile, bear left at the junction with Zion Hill Rd. Continue another mile until the road deadends into Buffalo Ridge Rd. (currently unmarked). Turn left and drive .4 mile to the Park entrance.

The Forest Preserve is currently undergoing extensive "development" by the Park District. A man-made lake, paved walkways and additional parking lots have been added. An old, rustic barn has been leveled but the shelter house, which yields a broad view of the Great Miami Valley, still sits at the top of the ridge. Park in the lot adjacent to the Wood Duck Trailhead.

Wood Duck Trail. This 1.3 mile hike meanders through a mixed woodland, skirting a meadow and crossing other small clearings along the way. The trail's destination is a secluded pond, surrounded by forest and partially rimmed with a marsh.

Mallards, wood ducks and herons feed at the pond during the warmer months. Mammals, including white-tailed deer, raccoons, opossum and an occasional fox may be spotted here at dawn or dusk. Salamanders and crayfish inhabit the creek, below the dam, while frogs haunt the marshy shores.

The area is especially beautiful in spring when redbud trees dapple the woodland and numerous wildflowers adorn the trail. Honeysuckle, multiflora rose and wild grapes have invaded the forest, providing food and shelter for wildlife but threatening the welfare of native plant species. Pockets of red cedar, among the first trees to reclaim "disturbed" areas, will be noted along the clearings.

Return to the parking lot via the same route.

The Wood Duck Trail

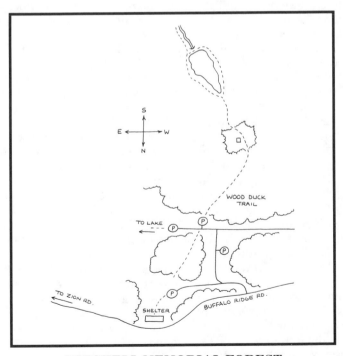

S

E ←→ W

N

WOOD DUCK
TRAIL

TO LAKE

TO ZION RD.

BUFFALO RIDGE RD.

SHELTER

MITCHELL MEMORIAL FOREST

14 SPRING GROVE CEMETERY

Distance: 3.8 miles
Terrain: rolling

Most of us do not think of a visit to the cemetery as a pleasant way to spend an afternooon. However, a stroll through Spring Grove, rich in history and natural beauty, is certainly an enjoyable experience. Initially conceived by Dr. Daniel Drake and designed by Howard Daniels, land was set aside for burials in 1845. The Cemetery has since gained national recognition for both its interred citizens and its spectacular landscape. Indeed, Spring Grove has been designated a National Historic Landmark.

Sprawling over 733 acres of wooded hillside, this is the largest private nonprofit cemetery in the United States. To reach Spring Grove follow I-75 and take the Mitchell Ave. Exit (Exit #6). Turn west on Mitchell and then south (left) on Spring Grove Ave. The Cemetery entrance will be approximately ½ mile on your right. A complete map of the grounds is available at the gate house.

Park in the lot adjacent to the old Administration Building (1). This Gothic structure dates from the mid 1800's. Walk through the tunnel and bear right, following the green-lined roadway. One of the first recognizable names is the gravesite of the Carew family (2), near Sylvan Pond (3). Farther on your left, bald cypress trees line the shore of Cedar Pond (4), their "knees" rising above the water's surface. On your right is the family mausoleum of Judge Jacob Burnet (5), a U.S. Senator and author of Ohio's first Constitution.

Angle left from the green road to see the tomb of Nicholas Longworth (6) whose vineyards sprawled across Mt. Adams (then Mt. Ida) in the early 1800's. He resided in the Martin Baum House which would later become the Taft Museum.

Return to the green road, wind uphill a short distance and then angle onto the drive that loops past the White Pine Chapel (7). Continue along this drive until it deadends into the white-lined road. Turn right, following the white road as it winds higher into the Cemetery.

After walking approximately ¼ mile you will pass between a woodland (8) and a pond (9). Bear right along the white road as it runs atop a ridge, yielding a broad view to the south.

At the next intersection turn left onto the yellow-lined road. Walk a short distance and continue straight ahead on the unmarked drive (see map). Continue on this road which eventually curves up to the right, ascending to Spring Grove's overlook (10). From the overlook one has a beautiful panorama of the Cemetery, the Mill Creek valley and the hills beyond. University of Cincinnati buildings poke above the Clifton Ridge. The view is' especially impressive in October, when fall colors blaze across the valley.

Descend from the overlook, pick up the white road and then switch to the yellow road just past the pond (11). Continue along the yellow road, crossing another pond (12) and passing through an open section of the Cemetery. Lower on the hillside the clustered monuments resume, including the grave of William H. Alms (13).

Turn left between Willow Water (14) and Maketewah Pond (15). Mute swans, Canada geese, mallards and migrant waterfowl are often found in this area. The grave of Andrew Erkenbrecker (17), founder of the Cincinnati Zoo, is located just north of the Cascade Pool (16).

*Bald Cypress trees line the
shore of Cedar Pond.*

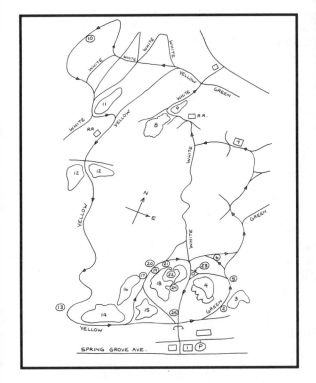

SPRING GROVE CEMETERY

Continue along the northern rim of Geyser Lake (18). On your right is the grave of Charles W. West (19), founder of the Cincinnati Art Museum. Across from the West monument is the tomb of Salmon P. Chase (20), former U.S. Senator, Ohio Governor, Secretary of State for President Lincoln, and Supreme Court Justice.

Farther along is the ornate, Gothic Revival mausoleum of the Dexter family (21), built in 1869. Adolf Strauch, Spring Grove's superintendent and landscape architect from 1855 to 1883, is buried on the island (22) in Geyser Lake.

Turn right, descending along the white-lined drive. On your left is the Soldier's Monument (23). Cast in Munich, Germany, in 1865, this bronze statue honors Cincinnatians who died in the Civil War. To your right, the Fleischmann tomb (24), modeled after the Greek Parthenon, sits along the northern shore of Geyser Lake. Near the bottom of the slope is the grave of General William H. Lytle (25), adorned with an eagle and laurel-draped column. He is one of 37 Civil War Generals buried here.

Pass through the tunnel and return to the parking lot. Your walking tour of Spring Grove Cemetery has totalled 3.8 miles.

15　MILFORD

Distance: 2.4 miles
Terrain: rolling

Situated along the eastern edge of the Cincinnati metropolitan area and separated from nearby communities by the Little Miami River, Milford, incorporated in 1836, has retained a small town atmosphere. First settled in 1796, the village's economy was based on lumber and grist mills well into the 1900's. Even today, the River plays a major role in Milford's commerce, attracting tourists and canoeists to the area.

To reach Milford from Cincinnati, follow U.S. 50 (Columbia Parkway) east. Drive 15 miles into Milford's central business district and leave your car at Riverside Park, also called Carriage Way Park (1). The Park offers an overlook of the Little Miami River and contains a small cemetery plot (2) with graves dating from the mid 1800's. A dam, which diverted water into the town's mills, used to span the river near the south end of the Park.

Walk south along High St. The Medaris House (3), at 512 High St., renovated during the 1970's, was originally built in 1811. Turn right onto Main St. and descend into the business district. Many of the shops that line these streets occupy structures that date from the early-mid 19th Century. Milford's oldest frame house (4), at 208 Main St., was built in 1809. The building at 114 Main (5), formerly the home of the Milford Historical Society, dates from 1817. The Ernst Building (6), on the northwest corner of Main and Garfield, was completed in 1849 and served as the city's first Masonic Temple.

Turn right along Garfield Avenue. When the village of Milford was first laid out, in 1806, this was titled "Cross St." It was later renamed to honor President Garfield. Turn left on Water St. which was

paralleled by a sluice during the city's milling era. The last of the grist mills, which burned down on New Year's Day, 1920, stood near the River, just downstream from the U.S. 50 bridge. On the northeast corner of Water and Mill Sts. is the Millcroft Inn (7). Built in 1816, it was the home of the John Kugler family from 1827 through 1868. Kugler, who installed Milford's first central heating system in this house, managed a mill, distillery, livery stable and general store on his riverside estate. Today, the Millcroft Inn is a popular restaurant and tavern known throughout the Tristate.

Milford's modern bridge (8), paralleling the 1925 steel structure (9), is actually the city's fourth bridge. The original span, constructed in 1818, was a wooden toll bridge.

Turn left along Mill St. The stone buildings clustered near the intersection of Mill and Main Sts. were all built by John Kugler. The "Corn House," (10), now called the "Old Mill Building," was used to store and process corn prior to its use in the production of whiskey. Continue along Mill St. which ascends into one of Milford's most attractive residential areas. Restored Victorian homes, some dating from the mid 1800's, line the shaded avenues. Turn right on Mound Ave. At Mound and Hickory is the entrance to the S.E.M. Villa Retirement Community (11). The Villa itself, constructed in 1929, was originally a Jesuit seminary. The seminary closed in 1969 and the property was acquired by the Southeastern Ecumenical Ministry, an organization of seventeen regional Churches. With the aid of a grant from H.U.D., the Ministry remodeled the Villa in 1971, creating 155 residential units. Since then, other buildings have been added to S.E.M.'s retirement community.

Walk east on Hickory and then north along Cleveland Ave., returning to Mill St. Turn left on Mill St., right on High St. and left on Garfield Ave., into town. Follow Main St. north through the business district. The Craver-Hookom

A crisp day on Cleveland Avenue

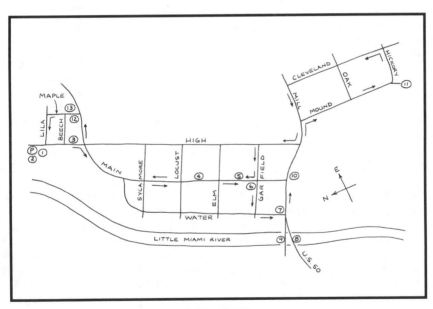

MILFORD

Funeral Home (12), at Main and Maple Sts., dates from 1870. Across Maple St. is the Milford Methodist Church (13), which has occupied the site since 1936.

Turn left (north) along Maple St. and then left on Lila Avenue, returning to Riverside Park. Your walking tour of Milford has totalled 2.4. miles.

16 CINCINNATI NATURE CENTER

Powel Crosley Lake Trail
  Distance: .8 miles
  Terrain: mostly flat; few hills

Lookout Trail
  Distance: 2.0 miles
  Terrain: rolling; few steep areas

If you enjoy a walk through the woods but cannot tolerate the untamed wildness, overgrown trails and "no facility" status of many nature preserves, we recommend a visit to the Cincinnati Nature Center. Established in 1967, the Center now encompasses 750 acres of forest, meadow and open woodland. Well-marked, manicured trails lead from the parking area to all sections of the preserve. The Rowe Interpretive Center houses refuge offices, an exhibit hall and a nature-oriented bookstore.

Numerous trail routes wind through the preserve and a complete map is provided by the Center. For an overview of the area, we suggest the following two hikes.

Powel Crosley Lake Trail. Perhaps the most popular hike at the Nature Center, this .8 mile loop starts behind the Interpretive building where a boardwalk straddles the western edge of Powel Crosley Lake. The trail then winds in and out of the adjacent forest as it circles the lake. Spur trails lead to the marshy shores where nature watchers can enjoy the myriad of creatures that inhabit this wetland.

Canada geese, mallards and red-winged blackbirds nest along the lake, wary of minks that patrol the marsh. Pied-billed grebes are often seen here during migrations and pileated woodpeckers roam the forest throughout the year. Frogs, snails and whirligig beetles entertain children from May through September.

Refer to the map which illustrates the trail's specific route. Trail intersections at the Nature Center are designated by numbered markers, making the maps easy to follow.

Lookout Trail. For a bit of solitude and diversity, try the Lookout Trail, most of which lies northeast of Tealtown Rd. (see map). This 2 mile route begins just across from the Center's entry road where it first skirts a large hayfield. After walking approximately 200 yards you will find a marsh-lined pond on your left. Numerous creatures are drawn to this oasis, especially during the spring and summer months.

Continuing eastward, the trail crosses the open fields and winds along the edge of a forest. It then angles to the north, snaking along the ridgetop. Several overlooks provide changing views of the East Fork Valley. A section of I-275 (near its junction with U.S. 50) can be seen in the distance. During the warmer months, turkey vultures soar along the ridge, lending a touch of wildness to the scene.

The return route winds through a mature forest, re-crosses Tealtown Rd., and climbs back to the parking area. This section of the hike is a bit hilly but the footing is good and short stairways help one negotiate steep areas.

To reach the Cincinnati Nature Center, follow I-275 to the east side of the city. Take the Batavia Exit (Exit #63-B) and head east on Ohio Route 32. Drive 1.2 miles to the stoplight and turn left on Gleneste-Withamsville Rd. Drive .4 mile, turn right on Old S.R. 74 and proceed ¼ mile to Tealtown Rd. Turn left and drive approximately 3 miles to the Center's entrance.

The Nature Center is open to the public on weekdays but is reserved for members on weekends and holidays. Membership is currently $25.00/year ($50.00/year for families). For more information see the Center's listing in the Appendix of this book.

Powel Crosley Lake

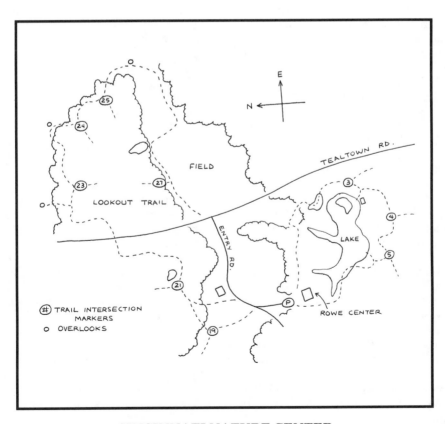

E
N ←

TEALTOWN RD.

FIELD

LOOKOUT TRAIL

ENTRY RD

LAKE

ROWE CENTER

#⃝ TRAIL INTERSECTION
MARKERS
○ OVERLOOKS

CINCINNATI NATURE CENTER

17 TERRACE PARK

Distance: 3.2 miles
Terrain: flat

The Terrace Park area was first settled in January, 1789, when Captain Abraham Covalt and a contingent of 45 adventurers arrived from Pittsburgh, Pennsylvania. Covalt constructed a fort ("Covalt Station") on the current site of St. Thomas Episcopal Church (7). Created to protect the settlers from local Indians, the fortress offered limited security ... Covalt himself was killed by Indians and the area's population remained sparse through the early 1800's. Completion of the Little Miami Railroad, in 1840, spurred settlement of the region and, in 1857, the Great Robinson Circus adopted the village as its winter home.

The name "Terrace Park" was apparently assigned by Jacob Tigner, a local manufacturer, in the 1870's. The village was eventually incorporated in 1893.

Over the past century Terrace Park has evolved into an appealing neighborhood with wide, shaded avenues. While many of its trees were destroyed by a tornado in 1969, the village launched a five-year tree restoration project, leading to its designation as "Tree City, U.S.A" in 1986 and 1987.

Tucked in an elbow of the Little Miami River, Terrace Park's flat terrain, quiet streets and attractive homes guarantee a pleasant stroll. Park along Elm Ave. in front of the Elementary School (1). Across the street from the school is a house (2) that dates from 1869. Just north of this residence is Lindell Grove (3), home to Boy Scout Troop 286.

Walk north along Elm Ave., cross the bridge and angle left onto Park Ave. (see map). Continue 1 block and turn right along Western Ave. to Wooster Pike. This major road, part of U.S. 50, follows the route of an old Indian trail. The Pike opened as a toll road during the mid 1800's and remained such for over fifty years. Terrace Park's first school opened in 1830 and was located in the building where the Yankee Dollar Gift Shop (4) now resides.

Turn right along Elm Ave. Terrace Park's Community Center (5) occupies a former Baptist Church, built in 1892. Purchased by the village in 1922, the Center is used for council meetings and community functions.

Cross the bridge and angle left onto Terrace Place. The Village Green Memorial Park (6) will be noted on your right. Walk 1 block and turn right along Rugby Ave. In sequence turn left on Yale, right on Oxford and left on Miami Ave. Directly ahead of you is St. Thomas Episcopal Church (7). Built in 1907 by John Robinson as a memorial to his wife and daughter, the Church occupies the former site of a mission that was established here in 1870 by Charles Kellogg. A small plaque also commemorates the former presence of Covalt Station on this plot.

Circle to the left, following Terrace Place and Cambridge Ave. (see map). Turn right and walk south along Miami Ave. as it parallels the course of the Little Miami River. Continue for six blocks and turn right on Stanton Ave. Follow this street back to Elm Ave. and to your car. Your walking tour of Terrace Park has totalled 3.2 miles.

To reach Terrace Park from downtown Cincinnati, follow Columbia Parkway (U.S. 50) east. This road becomes Wooster Pike as it heads up the Little Miami Valley. Entering Terrace Park, turn right at Elm Ave. This intersection, controlled by a stoplight, is approximately 14.2 miles east of the downtown area.

The Village Green

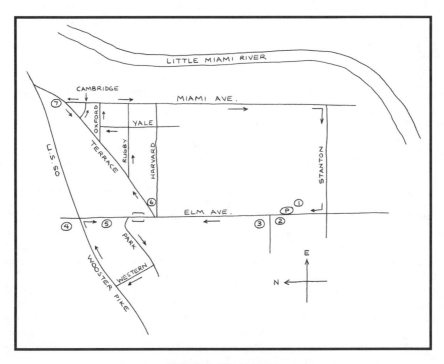

TERRACE PARK

18 MARIEMONT

Distance: 2.4 miles
Terrain: flat

Most towns and villages form gradually over many years as homesteads cluster near a convenient or attractive site. In contrast, Mariemont, east of Cincinnati, was conceived and almost totally planned by Mrs. Mary Emery and her family. Designed to resemble an Old English village, Mariemont's construction began in 1922. The village was eventually incorporated in 1941.

For a 2.4 mile walking tour of this clean and inviting community, park in the central square at the intersection of Wooster Pike and Miami Rd. At the west end of the square is the Mariemont Inn (1) which has served the village since 1926. A popular site for receptions and other social gatherings, the Inn's sixty overnight units are all unique in design and all furnished with antique furniture.

Follow Madisonville Rd. which angles to the northwest. Walk several blocks and turn left along Plainville Rd. The large, Italianate building on your left (2), complete with clock tower, is the Parish Center for the Mariemont Community Church. Completed in 1928, the building was originally the village recreation center. It was acquired by the Church in 1956 and now houses the parish offices, classrooms and a pre-school.

Turn right (west) on Chestnut St. The Dale Park Building (3), now a community education center, was first used as an elementary school when it opened in 1926. The Mariemont Community Church (4), dedicated in March of 1927, sits back from the southeast corner of Oak and Chestnut. Its tile roof, retrieved from a crumbling English monastery, dates from the early 14th Century.

Continue west along Chestnut St. and turn left on Beech. These blocks are lined with Tudor townhomes which characterize the older sections of Mariemont. Turn left along Wooster Pike,

heading back toward the square. The 50 acre Dogwood Park (5) sprawls along the opposite side of the Pike. Among the trees, a stone Bell Tower (6) rises 100 ft. Constructed in 1929, the tower was dedicated to Mrs. Emery.

The small War Memorial Cemetery (7) sits on a knoll, just south of the Community Church. Several of the graves date from the 1840's. Dale Park (8), south and east of the Cemetery, spreads to Plainville Rd. Mariemont Elementary School (9) occupies most of the next block. Completed in 1939, this building was the original home of Mariemont High School, which gave way to a Middle School in 1970. The Elementary School took over in 1983.

Continue east along Wooster Pike to the square. A plaque (10), at the west end of the square, commemorates the addition of Mariemont to the National Register of Historic Places in July, 1979.

Cross to the southeast corner of the square and follow Crystal Springs Rd. (see map). Angle left onto Mt. Vernon Ave. and then turn right along Miami Bluff Drive.

Across from the intersection of Miami Bluff and Center St. is a small park and stone concourse (11). The latter was dedicated to Isabella Hopkins and her sister, Mary Emery, in October, 1964. From the concourse the visitor has a broad view of the Little Miami Valley which stretches past the southern edge of the village.

Continue the walk along Center St., bear left onto West Center and then turn right along Miami Rd., which leads back to the square. At the east end of the square is a memorial to Thomas Emery (12), dedicated by his wife, Mary, in December, 1955.

To reach the village of Mariemont from Cincinnati, follow Columbia Parkway (U.S. 50) east. Columbia Parkway becomes Wooster Pike. Mariemont Square will be approximately 9.5 miles from the Downtown area.

Tudor townhomes line Chestnut Street

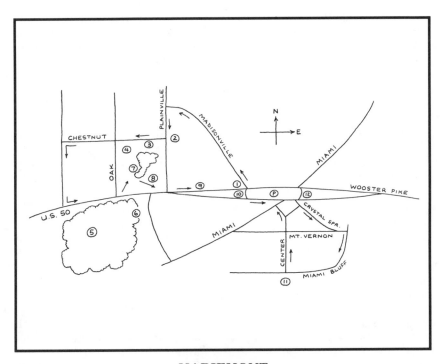

MARIEMONT

19   AULT PARK/OBSERVATORY HISTORIC DISTRICT

Distance: 3.0 miles
Terrain: rolling

Ault Park is one of Cincinnati's most popular and beautiful retreats. Its 236 acres, donated to the city by the Levi Ault family, spread across a ridge, bordering the Little Miami Valley.

To reach the Park, take I-71 to the Dana Ave. Exit (Exit #5). Turn east on Dana Ave. Crossing over Madison Rd., this street becomes Observatory Rd. which ends in Ault Park.

Park near the Pavilion (1) which is currently undergoing renovation. From its rooftop portico, one has a wide panorama of the Little Miami Valley to the east and of Ault Park's magnificent gardens, immediately west of the Pavilion. In the distance, University of Cincinnati buildings poke above the western horizon.

On the south side of the Pavilion is a memorial to Levi Ault (2), dedicated in 1911. Descend from this hillock and follow Observatory Circle around the north side of the gardens (see map). Bear right along Observatory Rd. which leads out of the Park. Re-entering the residential zone, proceed for a few blocks and turn right on Observatory Place.

This immediate neighborhood has been designated the Observatory Historic District. Victorian, Greek Revival and Transitional homes line the block, dating from 1877 to 1923. At the end of Observatory Place is the Cincinnati Observatory (3). Completed in 1875, the building's dome was reconstructed in 1895. It now houses a 16 inch refractor telescope, offices and an astronomical

library. It is open to the public by special arrangement only. Cincinnati's original Observatory, dedicated in 1843, was located at the top of Mt. Adams, the current site of the Holy Cross Monastery. The Observatory was moved to Mt. Lookout when the glow from our burgeoning city began to interfere with use of the telescope.

The smaller observatory, southeast of the main structure, is the Mitchell Building (4). Designed by Samuel Hannaford and Sons, it opened in 1908. It harbors an 11 inch telescope and is used for educational programs.

Walk along Avery Ct. (see map) to Wellston Place. Turn left along Wellston, cross Observatory Rd. and continue on Park Ridge Place. At Griest Ave., turn left for ½ block and then left again on Suncrest Dr. This street winds upward and eastward, intersecting Herschel Ave. Turn right along Herschel, passing John Kilgour Elementary School (5). Continue southward for a few blocks and turn left on Principio. This street leads back into Ault Park, entering along its southern ridge.

Near the Park entrance you are rewarded with a fine view of Lunken Airport to the south. Before returning to your car, stroll through Ault Park's beautiful gardens which offer one of Cincinnati's most spectacular floral displays from April through September,

Your walking tour through the park and its nearby scenic neighborhoods has totalled 3.0 miles.

The Cincinnati Observatory

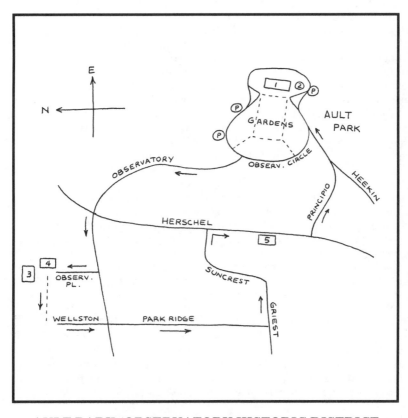

AULT PARK/OBSERVATORY HISTORIC DISTRICT   43

20 HYDE PARK

Distance: 2.8 miles
Terrain: rolling

Hyde Park, with its attractive homes, shaded streets and upscale shops, is certainly one of our more popular and fashionable neighborhoods. Incorporated in 1896, the village was annexed by Cincinnati in 1903.

For a walking tour of Hyde Park's central corridor, park at the village square, located at the intersection of Erie Ave. and Edwards Rd. A small park, centered around the Kilgour Fountain (1), divides Erie Ave. as it crosses the Square. The fountain, dedicated in November, 1900, is a gift from the John Kilgour family. Mr. Kilgour, a prominent businessman and landowner during Hyde Park's development, was president of the Cincinnati Street Railway Company. At the southeast corner of the Square is the Engine Company No. 46 Firehouse (2), which has served the community since 1907.

Walk east along Erie Ave. At the corner of Erie Ave. and Shady Ln. is St. Mary's Church (3), built in 1917. Its Classic Bedford-stone construction was modeled after the Old English Gothic churches of the 13th Century. St. Mary's parish was established in 1898 and its school was founded by Monsignor Patrick Hynes in 1908.

Further east, on the northeast corner of Erie Ave. and Paxton Ave., is the Church of the Redeemer (4), an Episcopal congregation founded in 1908. Having earlier used the Town Hall at Michigan and Erie, the congregation moved to its current site upon completion of the Church in 1950.

Continue east on Erie Ave. and turn right on Grace Ave. Ahead of you, at Grace and Observatory, is the Hyde Park Community United Methodist Church (5). This English Gothic Church, completed in September, 1927, occupies the former site of the Mt. Lookout Methodist Episcopal Church which had been on

the corner since 1880. The latter congregation merged with the Hyde Park Methodist Episcopal Church during the 1920's, forming the present day congregation.

Walk westward along Observatory Rd. This street follows the route of a 1790's stage line, which stretched from Walnut Hills to Chillicothe, Ohio. Hyde Park School (6), at Edwards and Observatory, opened in 1900. It currently teaches grades K through 6.

Continue west on Observatory past several blocks of stately homes. The Cincinnati Country Club (7) flanks the western end of the road. Established in 1895, it is the oldest golf club west of the Appalachians. The Club, which encompasses 122 acres, was incorporated in 1903.

Turn right along Madison Rd. Wulstin Triangle Park (8) is on your right, wedged between Observatory and Erie. Across Madison Rd. is Withrow High School. (9). Opened in September, 1919, the school was originally called East Side High. In 1924 it was renamed in honor of John M. Withrow, retiring President of the Cincinnati School Board. The school's 27 acre campus, acquired by the Board in 1913, was once part of the Erkenbrecker estate. Withrow's bell tower and the nearby bridge date from the school's inception. The bridge was restored through the efforts of the Class of 1981 and was renamed in honor of Nora Mae Nolan, a former teacher at Withrow.

Turn right (East) along Erie Ave. and return to Hyde Park Square. Your walking tour of this vibrant neighborhood has totalled 2.8 miles.

To reach Hyde Park, follow I-71 to the Montgomery Rd./Dana Ave. Exit (Exit #5). Turn east on Dana Ave. and proceed to Madison Rd. Jog to the left, crossing Madison, and continue east on Erie Ave. to the Square.

Hyde Park Square

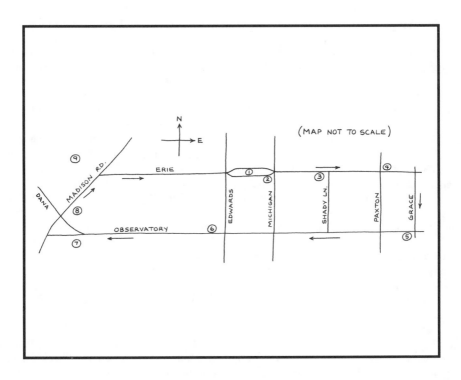

HYDE PARK

21 XAVIER UNIVERSITY/AVONDALE

Distance: 2.0 miles
Terrain: hilly; few steep areas

Xavier University was founded in 1831, at which time it was called the Athenaeum. Renamed St. Xavier College in 1840 (in honor of St. Francis Xavier) the school moved to its Avondale campus in 1919. Xavier achieved University status in 1930 and now offers more than 40 undergraduate majors in its three colleges. An all-male college for most of its existence, Xavier became co-educational in 1969.

The following 2 mile walk combines a tour of the University with a stroll through the adjacent neighborhood of Avondale. Park along Ledgewood Drive near Victory Parkway (see map). Walk north along Ledgewood, ascending into the hillside community.

Avondale has perhaps had more names than any other area in the city. After purchasing the land in 1802, William McMillan called the area his "Home Plantation." James Cory named the ridge "Locust Grove" when he assumed title but "Clintonville" was the accepted name by 1852. After much of the land was acquired by the Cincinnati & Chicago Railroad, H.C. Freeman, engineer and surveyor, was sent to inspect the area. It was he who bestowed the name of "Avondale" in 1854. The village had been incorporated in 1853 and was eventually annexed to Cincinnati in 1896. Following annexation, an influx of residents from the Cincinnati basin led to rapid growth of the neighborhood.

Angle left onto Avondale Ave. and then bear left along Winding Way. Walk 1 block and turn right, climbing higher into Avondale via Lenox Place. This attractive neighborhood is characterized by huge, castle-like homes, spacious, shaded lawns and wide, gas-lit streets. It has long been home to prominent Cincinnatians, offering a green, urban retreat above the industrialized valleys.

Near the top of the ridge, turn left on Redway Ave., descending toward Victory Parkway. Walk 1 block and turn right along Dakota Ave. which ends at Dana Ave. Turn left on Dana and descend further to Victory Parkway. One of our city's more attractive boulevards, the Parkway is adorned with flower beds during the warmer months.

Turn left (north) along Victory Parkway. Corcoran Field, former home of Xavier's football team, was recently demolished and the site (1) will be utilized for soccer and other field sports. Continue north to the Rev. Paul O'Connor Sports Center (2), which opened in 1976. This complex houses a swimming pool, basketball courts, weight room, handball and volleyball courts.

Cross Victory Parkway and ascend the stairs to Xavier's central campus area. Hinkle Hall (3) and Alumni Hall (4) are the University's oldest buildings, completed in 1920. Walk south along the front of these buildings for a sweeping view of the Avondale ridge to the west.

Angle left around Alumni Hall and walk north through the University Mall. The McDonald Library (5), on your right, opened in 1967. Further along, a statue of d'Artagnan (Charles II DeBatz Castelmore) graces the entrance to Albers Hall (6). D'Artagnan was a Captain-Lieutenant with the first company of Musketeers who died in the service of King Louis XIV of France, in 1673. The statue (7) was sculpted in Auch, France, and was a gift to the University by the Class of 1962. Xavier adopted the Musketeer mascot in 1925.

Continue northward through the mall, past Alter Hall (8), completed in 1960 and the Logan Chemistry Building (9), which opened in 1953. Bear to the right, walking

The University Mall

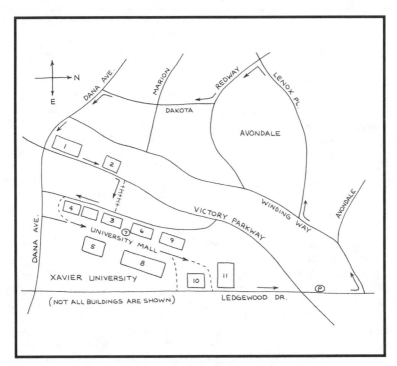

XAVIER UNIVERSITY/AVONDALE

between the St. Robert Bellarmine Chapel (10), dedicated in 1962, and the University Center (11), completed in 1965. Turn left along Ledgewood Drive and return to your car.

To reach Xavier University follow I-71 to the Montgomery Rd./Dana Ave. Exit (Exit #5). Drive west on Dana Ave. for approximately 1 mile and turn right on Ledgewood (see map).

22 CLIFTON

Distance: 5.2 miles
Terrain: rolling

With its stately homes and gaslit streets, Clifton is one of Cincinnati's most prestigious neighborhoods. First owned by Charles Clarkson, a Cincinnati merchant, most of the land north of Ludlow Ave. was then known as Clifton farm. During the mid 1800's, the land was subdivided into large estates as the first "Clifton Barons" settled in the area. Among this group were George McAlpin, James Hughes and Henry Probasco. The village was incorporated in 1850 and was eventually annexed by Cincinnati in 1896.

Our 5.2 mile walking tour through Clifton begins at Mt. Storm Park, which was purchased by Cincinnati in 1911. Accessed via Lafayette Ave., this urban refuge is a popular spot for picnics. Mt. Storm's location, at the western end of the Clifton ridge, yields a broad view of the Mill Creek Valley.

Leave your car in the Mt. Storm parking lot and backtrack along Lafayette Ave. The "Temple of Love" (1), on the Park's central knoll, dates from the mid 1800's. It was designed to cover a water pump though the latter was never used. Further along Lafayette, the castle-like Bethesda Home for the Aged (2) is perched along the ridge. Formerly known as the Scarlet Oaks Mansion, this 1867 structure was the home of George K. Schoenberger.

Turn right along Middleton Ave. which dips through the west side of "Old Clifton." Rawson Woods (3), a 10-acre Bird Preserve, occupies the northwest corner of Middleton and McAlpin Avenues. Cross McAlpin, proceed 2½ blocks and turn right on Evanswood. Walk 1 block and turn left along Whitfield, which jogs to the right, crossing Ludlow Ave. Ludlow is the business corridor of the Clifton area, lined with shops and restaurants.

Continue south on Whitfield and then turn left on Terrace Ave. Cross Clifton Ave. and wind into the northern end of Burnet Woods (see map). Good Samaritan Hospital (4) looms to the west of the Park. Founded in 1852 by the Sisters of Charity, the Hospital moved to Clifton in 1915. Just south of Good Samaritan is the Hebrew Union College (5), established in 1875 by Dr. Isaac M. Wise. It is the oldest Jewish theologic school in the western hemisphere.

Burnet Woods was set aside as a park in 1872. It has long been a haven for University of Cincinnati students and its artificial lake attracts fishermen throughout the year. The Trailside Museum (6) depicts flora and fauna that can be found in Cincinnati's Parks.

Exiting Burnet Woods, cross Jefferson Ave. and continue north along Brookline until it ends. Turn left on Glenmary and proceed to Clifton Ave. Immanuel Presbyterian Church (7), at Bryant and Clifton, dates from 1883.

Turn right (north) along Clifton Ave. The Church of the Annunciation (8), dedicated in 1929, offers an excellent example of Ionic style architecture. Further north, the Clifton Public School (9) fills the northwest corner of McAlpin and Clifton Avenues. Completed in 1905, the school is graced by the Probasco Fountain (10). The latter was dedicated in 1887, a gift to the village from Henry Probasco, who also donated Cincinnati's famous Tyler Davidson Fountain.

Calvary Episcopal Church (11), at 3766 Clifton Ave., was built in 1867. This Gothic structure's spire was yet another gift from Henry Probasco, a memorial to his brother-in-law, Tyler Davidson. The yellow, frame house at 3874 Clifton Ave. (12) is the former home of Robert Buchanan, President Buchanan's cousin, who moved to Cincinnati in 1823 and started a grocery business.

Turn left along Lafayette Ave. and proceed back to Mt. Storm Park, completing a scenic, historic and strenuous hike through Clifton.

The Temple of Love, Mt. Storm Park

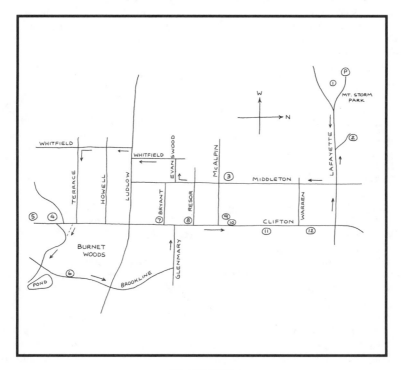

CLIFTON

To reach the Clifton area, follow I-75 and take the Hopple St. Exit (Exit #3). Turn left and follow Martin Luther King Drive as it winds up the ridge. Turn left (north) on Clifton Ave. and proceed to Mt. Storm Park, as per the map.

23 UNIVERSITY OF CINCINNATI

Distance: 2.0 miles
Terrain: rolling

The University of Cincinnati is certainly the academic hub of our city. Founded in 1819, the University moved to its Clifton campus in 1895. It now sprawls across 389 acres, including the Medical Center and branch campuses.

For a walking tour of U.C., take I-75 to the Hopple St. Exit (Exit #3). Follow Martin Luther King Drive east, winding up the Clifton ridge. Park along this road or on Brookline Drive in Burnet Woods (see map).

Walk south along Clifton Ave. The College of Design, Art & Architecture (1) sits on a hill to your left. Further along Clifton Ave. is Wilson Auditorium (2), completed in 1932. This hall is used for concerts and plays and has long been home to the Mummers' Guild, a U.C. drama company. The west side of Clifton Ave. is lined with sorority and fraternity houses.

Bear left and ascend along the semi-circular drive (see map). Near the top, turn left and climb the stairs to the front of McMicken Hall (4). This University building, the original on its Clifton campus, is named for Charles McMicken who, upon his death in 1858, willed his estate to Cincinnati for the creation of a municipal college.

Walk southward, crossing in front of the Old Van Wormer Library, (5), now the Administration Building. This structure dates from 1900. Continuing toward the south you will notice the towers of Hughes High School (6) in the distance. Dedicated in December, 1910, the building is one of Cincinnati's finest examples of Tudor architecture. The school is named for Thomas Hughes who left his estate to the city for the education of its poor children.

Just past the Teachers College (7), turn left and then right, passing in front of the Carl Blegen Library (8). This was U.C.'s main library prior to the opening of the Langsam Library (21) in August,

1978. Continue between the library and the Law School (9) and turn left along Corbett Drive as it descends from Calhoun St. Lined with nightclubs and cafes, Calhoun St. means recreation and relaxation for U.C.'s students.

The Patricia Corbett Pavilion (10) sits in a bowl to your left. This complex, dedicated in April, 1972, houses a 400 seat theater, renowned for its opera productions. Its $5 million construction was funded through the generosity of Mr. & Mrs. J. Ralph Corbett. At the bottom of the slope is Memorial Hall (11). This attractive, red-brick and stone building was completed in 1924. Ahead of you is Schmidlapp Hall (12), built in 1911, which now serves as the headquarters for the University's R.O.T.C. program.

Turn left, ascending onto the plaza that flanks Mary E. Emery Memorial Hall (13). The Hall and adjoining Corbett Auditorium (14) opened in November, 1967, celebrating the 100th anniversary of Cincinnati's College Conservatory of Music. This complex was also a gift from Mr. & Mrs. J. Ralph Corbett. Follow the plaza westward and then cross the elevated walkway as it angles to the right. The bridge and grassy slope that front Tangeman University Center (15) form the hub of student social activity during the warm days of spring and fall. The Tangeman Center, U.C.'s "Student Union," was completed in 1937.

Walk north on the path that zig zags along the west side of the Tangeman Center and then right, descending along the roadway (see map). On your left is the Renton K. Brodie Science and Engineering Complex. The building just across from Nippert Stadium (16) is James A. Rhodes Hall (17), named for Ohio's former governor who broke ground for the vast complex in 1964. Other buildings in the complex include Zimmer Auditorium (18), the Brodie Basic Science

The Tangeman University Center

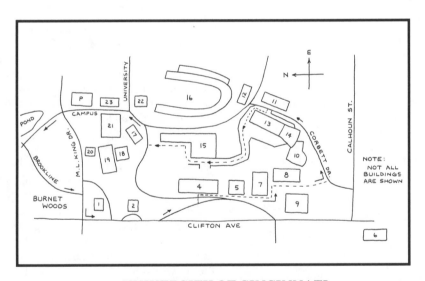

UNIVERSITY OF CINCINNATI

Center (19) and the Crosley Tower (20). The entire project took over six years to complete.

Nippert Stadium (16), home to the U.C. Bearcats, was completed in 1924. Continue down Campus Drive to University Ave. On your right is the new University Bookstore (22) and the Faculty Center (23). Ahead and to your left is the Walter C. Langsam Library. Dedicated in August, 1978, the building is named for

Dr. Langsam, President of the University from 1955 to 1971.

Walk north along Campus Drive, cross Martin Luther King Blvd. and enter Burnet Woods. Purchased by the city in 1872, the Park's 116 acres provide a welcome retreat for University students throughout the year. Turn left at the central intersection and follow Brookline Drive back to your car. Your walking tour of the U.C. campus has totalled 2.0 miles.

24 FAIRVIEW PARK

Distance: 1.7 miles
Terrain: hilly; steep sections

Except to local residents, Cincinnati's Fairview Park is relatively unknown. This is unfortunate since its 28 acres offer some of the most expansive views in the city.

Deeded to the Cincinnati Park Board in 1940, the Park stretches along the southwest terminus of Clifton Heights, 300 feet above the Mill Creek Valley. Though the latter is cluttered with railyards and industrial plants, it is, in fact, the heart of Cincinnati's economy. Beyond the valley, Price Hill and Mt. Airy fuse as a continuous ridge while, to the southwest, the Ohio River glistens in the sun. South of the Park, the downtown buildings rise from the Cincinnati Basin which is bordered to the east by Mt. Adams. Northern Kentucky's hills loom along the southern horizon.

To reach the Park from downtown Cincinnati, follow Central Parkway as it winds northward. Drive approximately 1.6 miles and turn right on W. McMillan Ave. Cross McMicken Ave. and watch for the Park's entrance on your right as you snake up the ridge. Park along this drive, near the playground (see map).

After enjoying the spectacular view of downtown Cincinnati, walk east along the Park's roadway. Turn left on Ravine St., one of our city's steepest streets. Walk ½ block and turn left along Warner St., ascending further up the ridge. At the top of the hill, turn left along Fairview Ave. and walk 1 block to another overlook of the Cincinnati basin.

Walk north along Fairview Ave. which eventually curves to the right and intersects McMillan Ave. St. Monica's Church, on your right, was completed in 1927. Constructed with Indiana limestone, the Church's 130 ft. tower is visible across much of the lower Mill Creek Valley. The building's interior is adorned with stained glass and paintings from Munich, Germany. St. Monica Church served as the regional Catholic cathedral during the renovation of St. Peter in Chains (1938-1957).

Cross McMillan Ave. and turn left along this heavily traveled road. Wind downhill and re-cross McMillan at the Park's entrance. Follow Scenic Drive which hugs the hillside and offers constant views to the south and west. Returning to your car, your walk through Fairview Park and Clifton Heights has totalled 1.7 miles.

View across The Mill Creek Valley

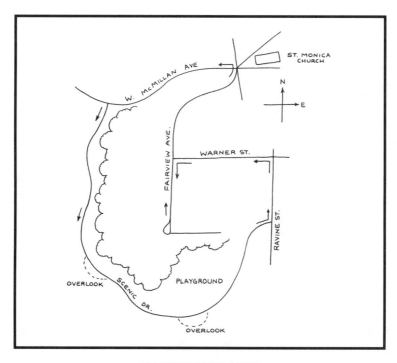

FAIRVIEW PARK

25 ALMS PARK/MT. LOOKOUT

Distance: 4.6 miles
Terrain: hilly; few steep areas

Alms Park, perched on a ridge above the junction of the Little Miami and Ohio River Valleys, is a terrific spot for a picnic. We suggest combining your picnic lunch with a pleasant hike through the adjacent neighborhoods of Mt. Lookout.

This area of Cincinnati was initially known as Spencer Township. Annexed by the city in 1870, it was renamed Mt. Lookout in 1875 when Cincinnati's Observatory was moved to the area from Mt. Adams. Today, the neighborhood's winding streets, shaded lots and attractive homes have drawn a new influx of residents. Modern houses hug the ridgetops, offering spectacular views, while older avenues, lined with stately homes, radiate from the central square.

To reach the area from downtown Cincinnati, follow Columbia Parkway (U.S. 50) east. Drive approximately 4.2 miles and turn left on Delta Ave. Ascend the hill for 1 mile and park in or near Mt. Lookout Square, formed by the intersection of Delta and Linwood Avenues.

Walk east along Linwood Ave., ascending a gentle hill. After hiking three blocks, turn right on Tweed Ave., following this road until it ends. Turn right on Kroger Ave. for ½ block and then left on Stanley Ave. Cross over Grandin Rd., continue for 1 block and turn left onto Vineyard Place. From this point to the Park, the route is devoid of sidewalks and, since the roads are winding and narrow, caution is advised. Vineyard Place curves along a ridgetop, its new homes endowed with superb views of the Ohio Valley.

Turn right on Tusculum Ave., descending for about ¼ mile to the Park's entrance (see map). The site of Alms Park was once known as Bald Knob, reflecting the fact that local Indians had cleared the summit for purposes of a lookout. The area was later called Tusculum Heights since it overlooked the riverside town of Tusculum. The Park itself, covering 85 acres, was donated to Cincinnati by Mrs. Frederick Alms in 1916, as a memorial to her late husband.

Follow the Park road, bearing right along the loop (see map). You will soon arrive at the Stephen Foster Memorial (1). This bronze statue, dedicated in 1937, commemorates the famous songwriter who spent several years in Cincinnati.

Proceed to the Park's Pavilion (2). From its upper portico one has a broad view of the Ohio Valley, backed by the Kentucky hills. The Park's east overlook (3) offers a spectacular view of the Little Miami Valley, including Lunken Airport. Children especially enjoy this panorama, entertained by the planes and helicopters that zoom across the valley. North of the Airport, the Little Miami Valley cuts into the southern Ohio countryside. Directly east, Mt. Washington stretches across the scene while the Ohio River curves in from the southeast, its waters often dotted with pleasure boats. The I-275 bridge spans the River, approximately 2 miles upstream from the Airport.

For those limiting their walk to the Park itself, the loop road is .5 mile in length. If you're heading back to Mt. Lookout Square, retrace your route along Tusculum, Vineyard Place, Stanley, Kroger and Tweed Avenues. At Linwood, turn right for ½ block and then left on Herschel Ave. Walk 4 blocks and turn left on Hardisty, which ends at Delta Ave. Turn left for a short walk back to the Square.

Celebrate! Your roundtrip journey has totalled 4.6 miles (and you've likely burned off that picnic lunch).

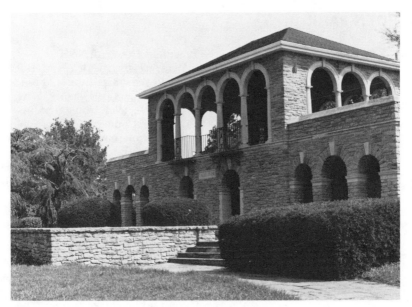

Alms Park Pavilion

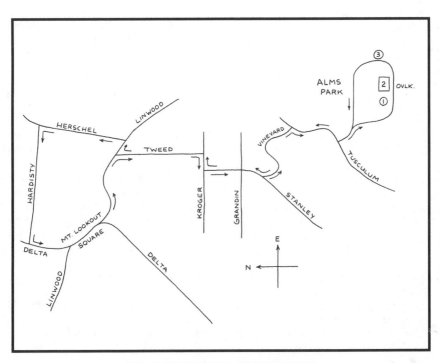

MT. LOOKOUT/ALMS PARK

26 EDEN PARK

Distance: 2.8 miles
Terrain: rolling; few steep areas

When Nicholas Longworth, one of Cincinnati's early land barons, planted his vineyards across the flanks of Mt. Ida, little did he know that his "Garden of Eden" would someday become one of America's premier municipal parks. Established in 1859, Eden Park spreads for 184 acres along this wooded ridge. A beautiful refuge for city dwellers, it is also home to several of Cincinnati's finest cultural attractions.

To reach the Park from downtown Cincinnati, head east on Columbia Parkway (U.S. 50). After passing I-471, stay to the right and exit onto the narrow, concrete viaduct that circles back across the Parkway. At the stop sign, turn right on Martin Drive and follow this road until it deadends into Eden Park Drive. Turn right, pass under the bridge and turn left on St. Paul Place. Park along this drive, across from the red-brick Water Tower (1).

This Tower, rising 172 feet, is visible throughout much of the Cincinnati area. It was constructed in 1894 to improve water flow to Walnut Hills. No longer used as a storage reservoir, the structure remains one of our most attractive and recognizable landmarks.

Before walking across the bridge, descend the slope to the Vietnam Memorial (2). Dedicated on April 8, 1984, the monument was designed by Ken Bradford and sculpted by Eleftherious Karkadoulious, who also restored the Tyler Davidson and President Garfield statues downtown.

Cross the concrete arch bridge and stop at the Eden Park Overlook (3), which offers a spectacular view of the Ohio River Valley. Dayton and Bellvue, Kentucky, are directly across the River and Ft. Thomas sprawls along the southern horizon. The Overlook's granite obelisk commemorates the canalization of the Ohio and marks the River's halfway point. The monument was dedicated by President Hoover in 1929.

Walk westward for about 100 feet and descend the stairs that lead to the Krohn Conservatory (4). Housing a vast array of plant life, from tropical palms to desert cacti, the Conservatory is open to the public throughout the year. Its warm confines and colorful flowers are especially inviting on a cold winter day.

Beyond the Conservatory a walkway crosses Martin Drive and heads westward, paralleling Eden Park Drive (see map). This route winds across an open garden, through a natural woodland and onto the lawn that surrounds Eden Park's reflecting pool (5). At the northwest corner of the lawn is perhaps the most photographed landmark in Cincinnati's Park system...the Spring-House. This gazebo (6) was initially built in 1905 to cover a natural spring. It now provides a shady rest-stop for park visitors.

Ascend from this basin, following Art Museum Drive (see map). You will soon pass the Bandstand (7), set in a natural amphitheater, where concerts and plays are often held during the warmer months. The present Bandstand was constructed in 1915, replacing the former 1872 structure.

Bear right at the top of the ridge for a walk past the hub of Cincinnati's art community...the Art Academy (8) and Art Museum (9). The Cincinnati Art Academy, founded in 1869, moved to Eden Park in 1887, where Frank Duveneck was its dean from 1888 to 1919. The Museum's central, limestone building was opened in 1886; several wings were added during the early 1900's.

Head back across the ridge and ascend further to Mt. Adams Circle, which loops around the Playhouse in the Park (10). Operated by the Tristate's only nonprofit, professional Theater company, the Playhouse first opened in 1960. The original Thompson Shelterhouse Theater seats 220 persons while the Robert S. Marx Theater, added in 1968, seats 629.

The Water Tower

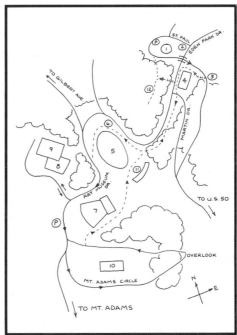

EDEN PARK

The Playhouse's eleven-production season, which runs from September to August, is funded through the Fine Arts Fund, the Ohio Arts Council and the National Endowment for the Arts.

An overlook at the south end of Mt. Adams Circle offers another view of the Ohio Valley. Continue around this drive and descend along the path that cuts past the Bandstand (see map) and leads onto the reflecting pool lawn. Stop by the retaining wall (11), part of Cincinnati's old reservoir system, for yet another expansive view to the south.

Re-trace your initial route to Krohn Conservatory (4) and cross Eden Park Drive, ascending a stairway to the Presidential Grove (12). Here trees have been planted to honor each U.S. President, starting with the George Washington oak, in 1882.

Walk north along the ridge, returning to your car. Your tour of Nicholas Longworth's "Garden of Eden" has totalled 2.8 miles.

Distance: .5 mile
Terrain: gentle hill; some steps

William Henry Harrison, the 9th President of the United States, was first introduced to southwest Ohio in 1791 when his military duties brought him to Fort Washington. Enamored with the region, he settled in North Bend in 1814. From there he directed his political and military careers. Elected to the House of Representatives in 1816, Harrison became a U.S. Senator in 1825 and was appointed Minister to Colombia in 1828. He was nominated by the Whig Party and elected President of the United States at the age of 68, the oldest first term President until Reagan's victory in 1980. Inaugurated in March, 1841, Harrison succumbed to pneumonia 1 month later, the first U.S. President to die while in office.

President Harrison's father-in-law was John Cleves Symmes, a wealthy New Jersey jurist and Congressman who claimed most of what is now Hamilton County. Judge Symmes founded the town of North Bend, convinced that it would serve as the nidus for settlement of the Ohio Valley. Later floods would prove him wrong and the higher, drier Losantiville site gave rise to the urban center. Despite this misjudgment, Symmes' extensive land holdings ensured that he would have a profound influence on the area's development, as road, township and community titles still attest today.

A short walk across a hillside in North Bend takes the visitor back to our city's infancy and pays tribute to these historic men. To reach the area, follow U.S. 50 (River Rd.) west from Cincinnati. Drive approximately 15 miles and turn right on Miami Ave. (watch for the sign directing you to the Harrison Memorial). Drive 1 block and turn left on Brower Rd. Proceed approximately ½ mile and turn right on Cliff Rd. Park in the small lot at the Memorial (see map).

Ascend the stairs and circle the monument (1) that rises above the tombs of William Henry Harrison and several of his family members. The elevated terrace overlooks the great North Bend of the Ohio River and the Kentucky hills beyond.

After circling the Memorial site, walk north along Cliff Rd. Approximately 50 yards up the slope a memorial to Abraham Brower (2) and a remnant of a 1796 mill stone (3) will be noted to the right of the roadway. Across from these monuments a stone stairway ascends into Congress Green (4), a small cemetery containing the grave of John Cleves Symmes (1742-1814) and other early settlers. Symmes' daughter, Anna, wife of William Henry Harrison, is also buried here. The central tomb, marked with a limestone obelisk, is the burial place of Betsy Basset Short, President Harrison's daughter, who died in 1846.

Returning to the parking area, your walk through history has totalled .5 mile.

The Harrison Memorial

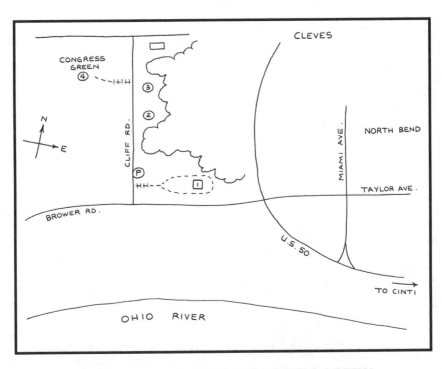

HARRISON MEMORIAL/CONGRESS GREEN

28 SHAWNEE LOOKOUT PARK

Miami Fort Trail
    Distance: 1.5 miles
    Terrain: hilly; few steep areas

Little Turtle Trail
    Distance: 2.0 miles
    Terrain: hilly; few steep areas

Blue Jacket Trail
    Distance: 1.3 miles
    Terrain: hilly; few steep areas

The Shawnee ridge, rising east of the lower Great Miami Valley, is rich in human history. Long before the first white men reached the Ohio River, Indian tribes had settled along this ridge. Providing broad views of the surrounding countryside, this forested retreat offered an ideal base camp. Hunting parties found abundant game in the forest and nearby marshlands. Fish were plentiful in the Ohio and Great Miami Rivers and these streams provided access to outlying areas.

The ridge was probably first used by Paleo-hunters over 15,000 years ago. These nomadic people crossed from Asia during the Pleistocene Epoch and traversed our continent in pursuit of mammoths, buffalo and other game. They were followed by Archaic civilizations, based on a forest subsistence and more inclined to remain in one area. Among these later groups were the "mound builders" who settled along the Mississippi and Ohio Valleys. In southern Ohio, they were represented by the Hopewell and Adena cultures. Hopewell Indians lived on the Shawnee ridge from about 300 B.C. until 450 A.D. Much later, probably in the late 1600's, modern tribes, including the Miami and Shawnee, arrived in the Tristate region.

Remnants of these Indian cultures persist along the ridge today. Shawnee Lookout Park was established in 1967 to preserve these artifacts and to provide recreation for Cincinnatians. The Miami Purchase Association, founded in 1960, organized the effort to protect the natural and cultural riches of this historic area.

To reach Shawnee Lookout Park from Cincinnati, follow U.S. 50 (River Rd.) west for approximately 15 miles. Entering Cleves, Ohio, turn left at the stoplight (Mt. Nebo Rd.), proceed 1½ blocks and turn right on Miami St. Follow this road as it curves to the left and parallels the Great Miami River. Drive 4 miles to the Park entrance, on your left. Daily usage fee is $1.00 per vehicle (or an annual pass to all Hamilton County Parks can be obtained for $3.00).

Shawnee Lookout Park provides three excellent hiking trails. Trail guide brochures are available for each and can be obtained at the ranger station.

Miami Fort Trail (A). This 1.5 mile loop originates at the end of the Park's central roadway. After ascending through the forest, the trail enters a large clearing, bordered by earthen walls. Since reclaimed by vegetation, these are the remnants of an ancient Indian fortress, constructed by the Hopewell Tribe. Burial mounds, borrow pits and other relics from their culture can be found in the surrounding forest.

Continue straight ahead at the trail intersection and proceed along the western edge of the Shawnee ridge. Several overlooks are spaced along this section of the trail, providing fine views of the Great Miami Valley. The lakes, marshlands and floodplain forest that border the Valley's croplands are home to a wide variety of birds, mammals and other creatures. Numerous migrants visit these wetlands in the spring and fall. Efforts are thus underway to preserve the Valley (known as "the Oxbow") as a

60

Entering the Fort

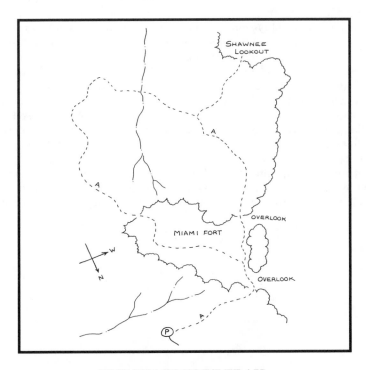

SHAWNEE
LOOKOUT

A

OVERLOOK

MIAMI FORT

OVERLOOK

A

W
N

A

P

THE MIAMI FORT TRAIL

wildlife refuge, free from further industrial development. Spearheaded by Oxbow Inc., local conservationists are working to protect the area by purchasing key tracts of land. For more information on this vital project see the Oxbow Inc. listing in the Appendix.

At the south end of the loop a spur trail leads out to "the Shawnee Lookout". Here, over 300 feet above the River, the visitor is treated to a spectacular view of the Ohio Valley, the mouth of the Great Miami River and the Northern Kentucky hills. The I-275 bridge spans the Ohio just west of the State line.

Return to the main trail loop and turn right. The trail dips through a steep ravine and then curves back toward the north, winding through the forest. A visit at dawn or dusk is usually rewarded by the presence of white-tailed deer that emerge from the woods to browse in open areas. Once back at the Fort, pick up the entry trail and descend to the parking area.

Little Turtle Trail (B). This 2-mile trail starts behind a playground, just across the road from a parking lot (see map). Named for a Chief of the Miami Indian tribe, the well-marked trail enters the forest, angles to the left and soon skirts a large meadow, dotted with bluebird boxes.

After hiking approximately ½ mile you will come to an intersection where the old entry trail comes in from the left (see map). Continue straight ahead, winding into a ravine and up the other side. This section is a bit steep in places but the

footing is good.

At the top of the ridge you are treated to a broad view of the Ohio River Valley, unmarred by power plants or storage tanks. Other than an occasional barge or pleasure boat, the scene is pleasingly devoid of 20th century distractions.

When you must move on, hike westward along the ridge. The trail eventually curves to the north and returns to the trail intersection. Turn left and retrace your entry route to the parking area.

Blue Jacket Trail (C). Named for a Chief of the Shawnee Indians, this 1.3 mile trail starts west of the Park's central roadway, just behind a parking lot (see map). After a gentle descent through the forest, the path crosses a power-line clearing where deer often browse at dusk.

Re-entering the forest you will soon come to a fork in the trail. Bear left, hiking along the ridge and then crossing another power-line cut. Knifing into the woods, the trail winds into a ravine, crosses a small creek and ascends the opposite hillside. At the south end of the loop a clearing provides an expansive view of the forested hills that flank the Ohio Valley.

Angling to the north, the trail climbs higher and the forest opens again, yielding a spectacular view of the Great Miami Valley. As discussed in the Miami Fort narrative, the "Oxbow" wetlands before you are a vital refuge for migrant and resident wildlife.

Follow the ridge as it curves toward the northeast. Re-cross the power-line cuts and return to your car via the entry trail.

Overlook from Little Turtle Trail

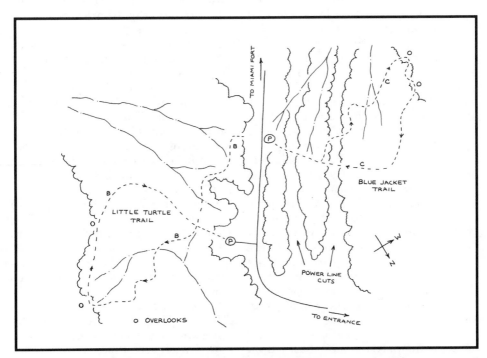

LITTLE TURTLE (B) & BLUE JACKET (C) TRAILS

29 SAYLER PARK

Distance: 3.0 miles
Terrain: mostly flat; few hills

Sayler Park, on the banks of the Ohio, has long been home to riverboat captains, tugboat crews and river lovers. First settled in the early 1800's, the town of "Home City" arose by 1849. Incorporated in 1879, the village was eventually annexed by Cincinnati in 1911. With annexation, the town's name was changed to Sayler Park, honoring Nelson Sayler, the town's first mayor. Annexation also encompassed the adjacent towns of Fernbank and Delhi.

For a walking tour of this riverside community, start at the village park, along Gracely Ave. The large home at 6624 Parkland Ave. (1), just north of the park, was built in 1880. The former home of Dr. Benjamin Lehman, it was originally planned as a hospital.

Walk east along Gracely Ave. for 1 block. The First Presbyterian Church (2), at Gracely and Twain, dates from 1867. To your southeast, the Twitchell House (3), built in 1860, sits behind a picket fence. Its former owner, Ernest Twitchell, invented the process of sapponification (used to make vegetable oil).

Head north along Twain Ave. to Home City Ave. The John McQuitty House (4), at 206 Twain, is one of the town's oldest homes. The McQuitty family donated the land for the village park. Turn west along Home City Ave. The Sayler Park Elementary School (5) was opened in 1929. Its 525 students range from kindergarten to sixth grade.

Continue west along Home City Ave. for approximately 1/3 mile, turn left on Dahlia Ave. and then right on Fernbank.

Short Woods golf course, on your right, encompasses 32 acres. An Indian burial mound (6) can be seen near the east end of the property.

Walk west along Fernbank Ave., a divided roadway. The town of Fernbank, founded by Charles Short, was incorporated in 1888. As discussed above, the village was annexed by Cincinnati in 1911, at which time it became part of Sayler Park. Turn left, descend along Overcliff and turn right onto Gracely Ave. On the hill to your right is the Church of the Resurrection (7), an Episcopal Church built by Charles Short as a memorial to his parents. Completed in 1877, the building's exterior was designed by Samuel Hannaford, the architect for Cincinnati's Music Hall.

Continue west to Thornton Park (8), a tiny, mid-intersection plot, centered by the Fitzhugh Thornton Memorial. The latter, dedicated in 1912, is the statue of an Indian, erected by Eliza Thornton to honor her deceased husband. With a total area of .01 acre, this is the smallest park in Cincinnati.

Return to your car by walking east along Gracely Ave. The Rudolph Siegel House (9), at 7128 Gracely, dates from 1903. Dr. Siegel was a pioneer in the field of endodontics. Take a well-deserved break at the park.....your tour has covered 3 miles.

To reach Sayler Park from Cincinnati, follow U.S. 50 (River Rd.) west. Drive approximately 10 miles and bear right onto Gracely Ave. Proceed 7 blocks to the village park.

The Fitzhugh Thornton Memorial

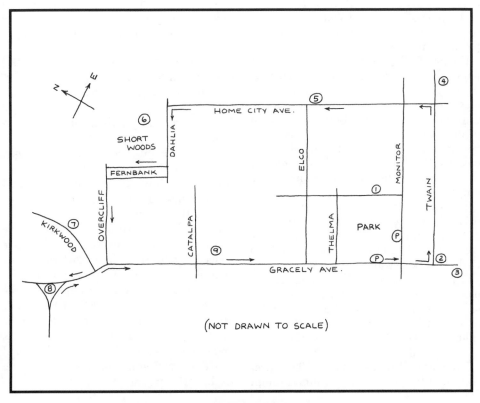

SAYLER PARK

Parcours Fitness Trail
   Distance: 1.0 mile
   Terrain: rolling

The term "fitness trail" usually brings to mind an oval, asphalt track, lined with chin-up bars. Embshoff Wood's Parcours route shatters that image, offering a pleasant hike through scenic terrain.

Embshoff Woods & Nature Preserve joined the Hamilton County Park District in 1982. It's 226 acres of forest and meadow stretch across a ridgetop in Delhi Township, approximately five miles west of downtown Cincinnati. Conceived by George and Margaret Embshoff, who donated the initial tract of land, much of the Preserve's territory remains in its natural state.

To reach the Preserve, take U.S. 50 (River Road) west from Cincinnati. Drive 2.5 miles and turn right on Fairbanks Ave. Proceed ½ mile and bear left onto Delhi Pike. Drive approximately 1.2 miles and turn left on Mt. Alverno Rd. Go one block and turn left onto St. Paul Rd. which leads into the Preserve. Park in the lot adjacent to the Parcours Trail, just across from the River Mount Pavilion (1).

Parcours Fitness Trail. The first section of this 1 mile hike winds through an open woodland, skirting the Park's frisbee golf course (2). Cincinnati's downtown buildings loom above the eastern horizon, providing a scenic backdrop.

Crossing a service road, the trail descends into a ravine. At the bottom, turn left for a gentle ascent of the next ridge. Along the western end of the loop the trail crosses a small meadow and then re-enters the forest. Hike eastward, descending a long series of earthen steps. At the bottom the trail loops back toward the west, following the stream bed, and re-joins the entry trail. Turn left and wind back to the parking area.

For those inclined to accept the challenge, eighteen exercise stations are spaced along the Parcours Trail. Bird enthusiasts will enjoy watching the hawks and kestrels that often soar above the meadow. Other wildlife at Embshoff Woods include great horned owls, barred owls, raccoons, opossum, gray squirrels and numerous songbirds. Their continued presence reflects the success of the Embshoffs' dream.

A blustery day on the Parcours Trail

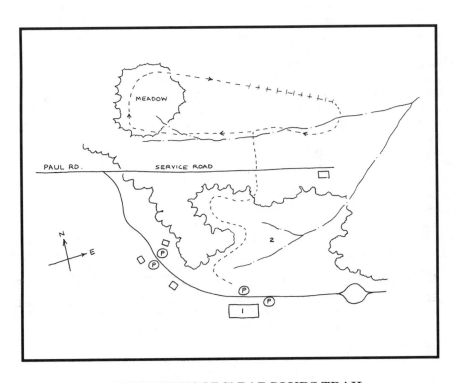

EMBSHOFF WOODS' PARCOURS TRAIL

67

31   MT. ECHO PARK

Distance: 1.25 miles
Terrain: rolling

Of all the promontories that overlook Cincinnati's downtown area, Mt. Echo Park, at the southern end of Price Hill, yields the grandest panorama. Established in 1908, the Park spreads for 73 acres across this high ridge. From its terrace, 300 feet above the Ohio River, the visitor is treated to an expansive view of the Cincinnati basin as it fans out from the lower Mill Creek Valley. Beyond the city's skyscrapers, the highlands of Clifton, Mt. Auburn and Mt. Adams appear to fuse as a continuous ridge. Across the Ohio, the Kentucky hills rise above the riverside communities. Barges and speedboats ply the river as trains, cars and trucks roll across the many bridges.

To reach the Park from downtown Cincinnati, follow 6th St. (U.S. 50) west. Keep right and exit onto Elberon Ave. which winds up the hillside. The Park entrance will be on your left, near the crest of the ridge.

Follow Mt. Echo Park Rd. until it ends in a parking lot, adjacent to a play area (see map). From the lot you will have a broad view of the Ohio River Valley as it curves south and west from the city.

Cut across the playground to the forest margin and find one of several entrances to the Park's nature trail (see map). This short path dips through a wooded ravine, traversing steep sections via rock stairways. Emerging from the forest, angle to the left and follow the wood's margin to a shelter (1) near the north end of the Park.

Cut back through the baseball field (2), cross Crestline Ave. and hike across the open woodland that rises gently from the road (see map). At the end of this low ridge is a stone shelter with four chimneys (3). Constructed by the W.P.A., the structure is a popular spot for family picnics. From its stone wall, the visitor has another view of downtown Cincinnati, framed by nearby trees.

Descend the stairs to Mt. Echo Park Drive and follow the road to the Park's famous overlook (4). During the warmer months, spectacular floral gardens adorn the Park's Pavilion (5). Newly renovated, this pillared landmark is utilized for a variety of social events.

Follow Mt. Echo Park Drive back to the parking lot, completing a walk of 1.25 miles.

View from Mt. Echo's Overlook

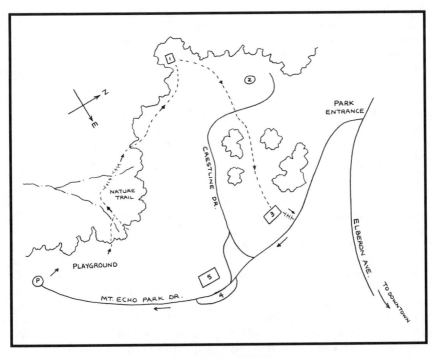

MT. ECHO PARK

32 OVER-THE-RHINE/LIBERTY HILL

Distance: 1.2 miles
Terrain: hilly; steep areas

In the mid 1800's German immigrants, attracted to Cincinnati by its booming economy, settled the area north of the Miami-Erie Canal, an area they nostalgically called "Over-the-Rhine." Unfortunately, a century later, this section of town began to decay as its middle class citizens departed for outlying neighborhoods. Its attractive brick homes, abandoned to the poor and dispossessed, started to crumble and the area became little more than a sprawling slum. Only a few businesses remained to preserve the German heritage of this once thriving community.

During the 1960's, an infusion of Federal funds initiated an effort to rejuvenate this historic district. However, the movement stalled until urban renewal became a political and economic necessity during the past decade. Most of the area's renovation is clustered near the northernmost blocks of Sycamore Street.

For a 1.2 mile walking tour of this revived neighborhood, park in one of the lots along Sycamore St. between 11th and 13th Streets. Walk north along Sycamore. The Diner (1), a popular bar and restaurant, opened in April, 1984. It is built around an authentic Mountainview Dining Car, constructed in 1955. The car was used in Massilon, Ohio, until it was moved to Cincinnati, in 1984.

On the northeast corner of 13th and Sycamore is the School for Creative & Performing Arts (2). Opened in 1977, the School occupies the old Woodward High School building which was constructed in 1910. Woodward High was actually established on this site in 1831, the first public high school west of the Appalachians. Named after its founder, surveyor and real estate magnate William Woodward, the school eventually moved to the Swifton area in 1953.

Continuing north along Sycamore you will pass Salem's Kirche (3). This Gothic-Revival structure was completed in 1867. Cross Liberty St. and ascend the hill for two blocks. Turn right along Boal St. After walking 1½ blocks you will reach a small park (4) which offers a spectacular view of downtown Cincinnati. Descend through the park and turn left (east) along Milton St. This appealing avenue is lined with renovated homes, most of which possess fine views of the city.

At the end of Milton St., turn right along Highland Ave., crossing to the east side for a broad view of the I-71 valley. Eden Park and Mt. Adams rise beyond the highway. To the south are views of the P & G towers, the I-471 bridge and Northern Kentucky's hills.

Bearing right, Highland Ave. becomes Liberty Hill and descends to Liberty St. Cross Liberty at Broadway and walk south past two blocks of revitalized rowhouses. Turn right on 13th St. and then left on Sycamore, returning to your car.

The large, dome-topped church at 12th and Spring Streets is St. Paul's Church (5). Completed in 1850, the Romanesque Church and its adjacent buildings are currently undergoing renovation. A boys school occupied the complex in 1862, followed by a girls school in 1908.

Rowhouses along Liberty Hill

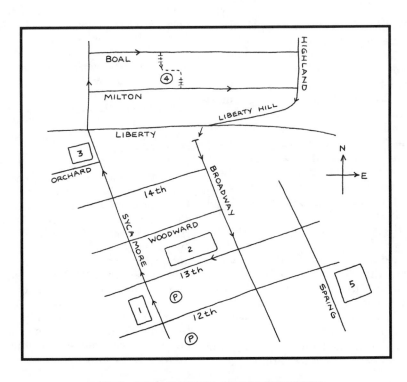

OVER-THE-RHINE/LIBERTY HILL

33 PLUM ST./CENTRAL PARKWAY/EIGHTH ST.

Distance: 1.8 miles
Terrain: flat

If you don't mind mixing religion and politics, the following walk will take you past some of Cincinnati's most impressive buildings. Park in one of the decks at 6th and Elm Sts. and walk north along Elm.

The Cincinnati Bell Telephone building (1) fills the southwest corner of 7th and Elm St. Established in 1878, the Company moved to this magnificent building in the early 1900s. Continue north along Elm to the Covenant First Presbyterian Church (2), at 8th and Elm Sts. Dedicated in 1875, this Church's congregation is a composite of four Presbyterian communities, the oldest of which dates back to 1790.

Turn left (west) on 8th St. and proceed 1 block to Plum. This is surely the most powerful intersection in Cincinnati. On the southeast corner is the Plum St. Temple (3). The Temple was constructed in 1866 and provides an excellent example of Moorish Revival architecture. Under the leadership of Rabbi Isaac M. Wise, it was the site of the first ordination of rabbis in America.

On the southwest corner of 8th and Plum is St. Peter in Chains Cathedral (4), completed in 1845. Its 200 foot steeple is visible throughout much of the Cincinnati basin. The Cathedral, spiritual center of our city's Roman Catholic community, was closed for renovation from 1938 to 1957. St. Monica Church, in Clifton Heights, served as the temporary cathedral during that time.

Cincinnati's City Hall (5) looms above the northwest corner. Dating from 1892, the Romanesque building's fine, red-granite stone work was supervised by David Hummel, who also built Scarlet Oaks (in Clifton) and the Eden Park Water Tower.

Walk north along Plum St. which soon merges into Central Parkway. This wide boulevard, completed in 1926, covers the route of the old Miami-Erie Canal and Cincinnati's ill-fated subway line. The Cincinnati-Dayton section of the Canal opened in 1827 but was closed by the early 1900's. Plans were then advanced to construct a subway through the old Canal bed. The futile work began in 1920 and the project was abandoned soon thereafter. Remnants of the subway still remain beneath the Parkway today.

Continue north along Central Parkway for 2 blocks and turn right on 12th St. On the northwest corner of 12th and Elm is the Apostolic Bethlehem Temple (6). This structure was formerly the St. John Unitarian Church, the first German-Protestant congregation in Cincinnati. Turn left (north) along Elm St. The Hamilton County Memorial Building (7), on your left, is a fine example of Beaux-arts Classical Revival architecture. Completed in 1908 and designed by Samuel Hannaford & Sons, the building was dedicated to pioneers and soldiers. Over the past 80 years it has been used for community meetings, concerts, graduation ceremonies and other cultural events. It is now home to the Miami

Cincinnati's City Hall

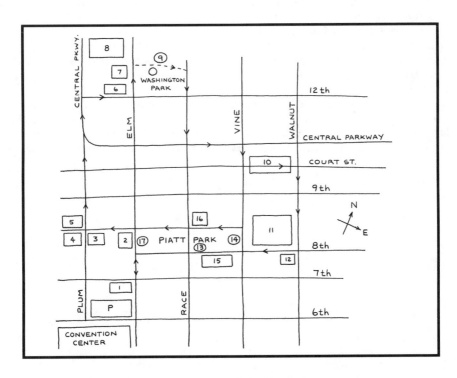

PLUM ST./CENTRAL PARKWAY/8TH ST.

Purchase Association which, founded in 1964, directs the protection and preservation of historic structures, neighborhoods and archaeological sites throughout the Tristate region. The building itself is listed on the National Register of Historic Places.

Continue along Elm St. to the grand entrance of Cincinnati's Music Hall (8). Designed by Samuel Hannaford, perhaps our city's most famous architect, this palatial building opened in 1878. Its construction was spearheaded by Reuben Springer, whose statue graces the Hall's foyer. Springer saw the need for a spacious concert hall where the German community could enjoy their regular music programs, especially the May Festivals. First held in 1873, the Festival remains the oldest, annual choral festival in the Americas.

Backtrack along Elm St. for ½ block and cut through Washington Park (9). Centered around a gazebo/bandstand, this urban park, acquired by Cincinnati in 1855, was initially the site of a Presbyterian cemetery. Walk south along Race St., turn left along Central Parkway and then right onto Vine St. Proceed 1 block and turn left, crossing through the Court Street Marketplace (10).

Turn right on Walnut St., passing Library Square (11) which fills the block between 8th and 9th Sts. The Public Library of Cincinnati & Hamilton County moved to this location in 1955 (it formerly occupied the Enquirer Building at 617 Vine). The Library underwent extensive renovation and expansion during the early 1980's and is now one of the most impressive public libraries in the country. Established in 1867, the central library coordinates 39 branch facilities throughout Hamilton County.

St. Louis Catholic Church (12) sits on the southwest corner of 8th and Walnut. This limestone, Florentine structure was dedicated in 1930. Walk west along 8th St., crossing Vine, and enter Piatt Park (13). Donated to the city by John and Benjamin Piatt in 1817, the Park stretches along 8th St. between Vine and Elm. A bronze statue of President James Garfield (14), first unveiled in 1887, now graces the east end of the Park. The Presidential Plaza (15), formerly the Doctors' Building, is currently undergoing renovation. Built in 1923, this Gothic Revival structure was added to the National Register of Historic Places in 1987. North of the Park is the Cincinnati Club (16). This impressive, limestone building was completed in 1924 and houses a wide range of club facilities. A statue of William Henry Harrison, on horseback, stands at the west end of Piatt Park (17). Dedicated in 1896, the statue emphasizes Harrison's long military service that preceded his political career.

Turn left (south) along Elm St. and return to the parking decks. Your walking tour has totalled 1.8 miles.

Music Hall from Washington Park

Garfield Statue at Piatt Park

Distance: 1.8 miles
Terrain: flat; some stairways

Cincinnati's extensive skywalk system, often praised by urban planning groups, debuted in 1972. This elevated walkway links many of the downtown buidings while providing an escape from the noise and congestion of city traffic. Along its route are many of Cincinnati's luxury hotels and several of her most famous landmarks.

Park in one of the decks at 6th and Elm Sts. Cross over 6th St. via the third-floor bridge, entering Cincinnati's Convention Center (1). Initially opened in 1967, the Center was expanded and renovated in the mid 1980's to keep up with the city's thriving convention business. The new, 165,000 square-foot complex, dedicated in 1987, was renamed in honor of Dr. Albert B. Sabin who developed the oral polio vaccine.

Cross Fifth St. to Convention Place Mall (2), home to a gallery of specialty shops. Follow the walkway eastward, crossing over Elm St., and enter the Hyatt Hotel (3). The Hotel's large, sun-lit piano lounge always invites a stop for refreshment.

Adjacent to the Hyatt is Saks Fifth Avenue (4). Continue east as the skywalk crosses Race St. and enters the Carew Tower block (5). Rising 48 stories above the city streets, the Carew Tower is Cincinnati's tallest building. It was completed in 1930 and has since been home to the Netherland (now Omni-Netherland) Hotel. Descend from the skywalk level and stroll through the building's central arcade for a true 1930's experience. If time permits, take an elevator to the Carew Tower's observation deck. From its lofty perch the visitor enjoys a spectacular view of the Ohio and Mill Creek Valleys.

Exit at the east end of the arcade, cross Vine St. and cut through the atrium of the Westin Hotel (6). Always bustling with activity, the Hotel opened in 1981. Its large atrium is often the site of cultural and holiday displays.

Directly across Fifth St. is Cincinnati's most famous landmark, the Tyler Davidson Fountain (7). Purchased in Bavaria, the Fountain was a gift to the people of Cincinnati from Henry Probasco. It was dedicated in 1871 and named in honor of Mr. Probasco's brother-in-law. The surrounding Square (8), enlarged and remodeled in the 1960's, is the site of free concerts, street fairs, political demonstrations and general relaxation throughout the year.

Walk east along Fifth St. The U.S. Post Office Building (9) fills the entire block north of Fifth between Walnut and Main. This impressive structure was completed in 1939. The Federal Building (10) and the Chiquita Center (11) occupy the next block. The latter, opened in 1983, is topped by a "weather beacon," the color of which signifies the following day's forecast.

Beyond Sycamore St. the Proctor & Gamble Plaza (12) sprawls toward the twin towers of P & G's office complex (13), completed in 1985. South of the Plaza, at Fifth & Sycamore, is the Taft Theater (14). Opened in 1928, this 2500 seat theater is the site of Broadway productions throughout the year. It was designed by Henry Hake and is named for Charles P. Taft, Cincinnati's famous philanthropist.

Turn left (north) along Broadway, cutting across the P & G Plaza to 6th St.. Turn left on 6th, walk 1 block and turn left on Sycamore St. (see map). Pick up the Skywalk in the Chiquita Center (11) and follow it westward. The walkway skirts Fountain Square and passes through open-air patios. At the Clarion Hotel (15), angle right, crossing 6th St., and then left, crossing Elm St. into the parking garage.

Your tour of Cincinnati's central business district has totalled 1.8 miles (excluding side trips that likely occurred along the way).

The P & G Towers loom beyond The Plaza

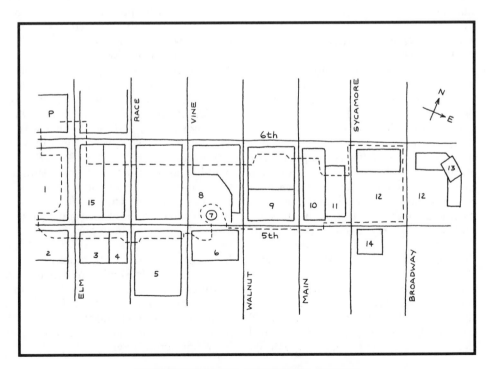

THE SKYWALK/FIFTH ST. TOUR

CINCINNATI RIVERFRONT/ LYTLE PARK HISTORIC DISTRICT

Distance: 2.6 miles
Terrain: mostly flat; few stairways

This walking tour of Cincinnati's Riverfront and the Lytle Park Historic District starts where our city began, at the Public Landing (1) along the banks of the Ohio. It was in this area that the first boat of settlers came ashore on December 28, 1788. They called their pioneer town "Losantiville", meaning "the village across from the mouth of the Licking River." As the city grew, the Public Landing became the hub of a thriving steamboat port. While most of the "tall stacks" have long since disappeared, Cincinnati's Delta Queen and the Showboat Majestic (2) still dock along this shore. The latter, built in 1923, is a permanent feature of the Landing and is used for theater productions during the summer months. Acquired by the city in 1967, the Showboat was added to the National Registry of Historic Places in 1980.

Leave your car at the Public Landing and walk east, crossing under the Central Bridge and entering Yeatman's Cove Park (3). Opened in 1976, the Park is named for Griffin Yeatman who operated the "Square & Compass" tavern near this site back in the 1790's. A unique feature of the Park is the Serpentine Wall (4), a contoured, concrete wall of steps, used for concerts and river watching. The Park itself is a popular spot for picnic lunches and is regularly used for festivals throughout the warmer months. Along the north edge of the Park is the Lytle Place Fountain (5) and wading area, a cool retreat on hot summer days.

Proceed eastward through the bricked "Skyline Arches" (6) beneath the L&N Bridge. Entering the "Bicentennial Commons at Sawyer Point" (7), you are greeted by a 12-foot statue of Cincinnatus (8), the Roman soldier and farmer after whom our city was named. The 22-acre Park opened in June, 1988, in celebration of Cincinnati's Bicentennial. Bear left along the north edge of the central lawn. The P&G Pavilion (9) is used for concerts and other performances during the warmer months of the year.

North of the Pavilion area is the main entrance to Bicentennial Commons. This includes the famous "flying pig sculptures" (10) and a flowing model of the Ohio River and its numerous locks (11). The Bicentennial Brick Promenade (12) stretches along the southern rim of the entry complex. Sponsored by the Kroger Co., this path of bricks, each imprinted with the name of a Tristate resident or family, created the opportunity to both fund the Park and purchase a "place" in the history of our city.

Continue eastward past the Fitness Area (13), Playground (14), volleyball courts (15), Lindner Tennis Complex (16), the Schott Amphitheater (17), all-weather skating rink (18) and the Boathouse (19). The latter houses a restaurant and an Olympic rowing center. The Schott Amphitheater preserves a section of Cincinnati's old waterworks plant.

Return along the walkway that parallels the riverbank (see map). Several overlooks and a fishing pier (20) jut over the water, providing views of the Ohio River and Northern Kentucky's hills. Pass through the Skyline Arches (6) and continue westward through Yeatman's Cove Park. Angle north to the Lytle Place Fountain (5) and ascend the stairs to the pedestrian bridge (21) that crosses over Ft. Washington Way.

Bicentennial Commons

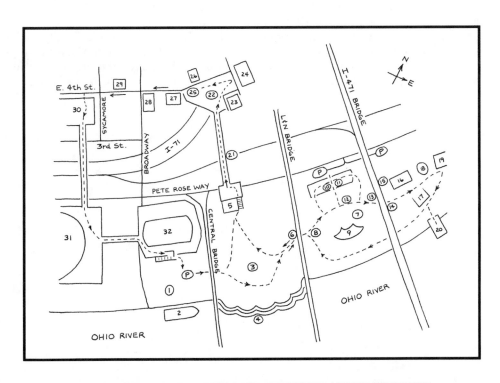

CINCINNATI RIVERFRONT/LYTLE PARK DISTRICT

Just north of the highway is Lytle Park (22), a beautiful, green oasis, purchased by the city in 1905. Spectacular floral displays adorn the park from April to October and shaded benches entice visitors during the heat of summer. On the southeast edge of the Park is the Anna Louise Inn (23), a residence and social center for young women since 1909. The Inn is named for the daughter of Charles P. Taft. At the east end of the Park is the Taft Musuem (24). Built in 1820 by Martin Baum, a local banker and manufacturer, the house was later occupied by Nicholas Longworth, whose vineyards cloaked the Mt. Adams ridge. Charles P. Taft purchased the home in 1900 and it was here that William Howard Taft accepted the Republican nomination for President in 1908. Charles Taft donated the house to the city of Cincinnati in 1932.

Near the west end of Lytle Park is a statue of President Abraham Lincoln (25), dedicated in 1917. It was yet another gift to the city from the Charles P. Taft family. Along the north edge of the Park, at 500 E. 4th St., is The Literary Club (26). Completed in 1820, this building provides an excellent example of Georgian style architecture. The Literary Club, established in 1849, moved to this site in 1875.

Walk west along E. 4th St. A plaque on the Guilford School building (27) commemorates the site of Fort Washington, a federal outpost that was instrumental in the early development of our city. The University Club building (28), at 4th and Broadway, dates from 1880. The Club itself was founded in 1879 and moved to this location in 1907.

Cross Broadway and continue west. Christ Episcopal Church (29), at 318 E. 4th St., was completed in 1835. Cross Sycamore St., continue ½ block and turn left into the Atrium I Building (30), just opposite the "Skywalk" sign. Cut through the center's attractive atrium and follow the walkway that crosses Ft. Washington Way (see map). Along the way, a history of baseball is presented via a series of overhead posters.

The walkway leads onto the plaza surrounding Riverfront Stadium (31). Home to the Reds and Bengals, the stadium opened on June 30, 1970. Turn left across the bridge that connects the stadium plaza with the Riverfront Coliseum complex (32). The Coliseum opened in September, 1975 and seats up to 17,800 spectators.

Descend to the Public Landing from the south side of Riverfront Coliseum (see map). Your tour of the city's riverside parks and historic Lytle Park District has totalled 2.6 miles.

The Taft Museum

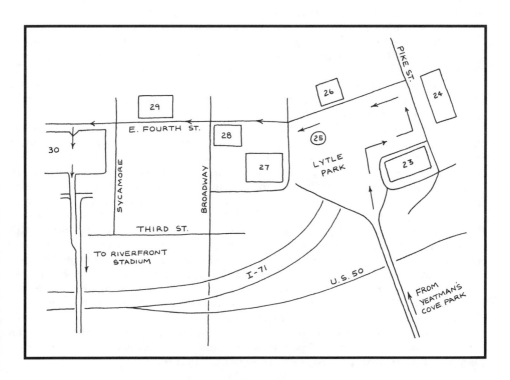

E. FOURTH ST./LYTLE PARK

36 MT. ADAMS

Distance: 1.4 miles
Terrain: steep hills

To Cincinnatians, "Mt. Adams" brings to mind steep, narrow streets, broad vistas, outdoor cafes and quaint shops. Indeed, perched high above the city's basin, Mt. Adams is one of the more unique communities in out metropolitan area. A walk through its hilly maze offers a pleasing blend of history and modern leisure.

To reach Mt. Adams follow Gilbert Ave. north and east from the downtown area (this avenue is the eastern extension of 7th St.). Drive approximately 1 mile and turn right on Eden Park Drive. Bear right onto Art Museum Drive and park in the gravel lot at the top of the ridge (see map).

Walk south along Ida St. Mt. Adams was originally called "Mt. Ida" and was the site of Nicholas Longworth's extensive vineyard. The ridge was renamed "Mt. Adams" in 1843, honoring President John Quincy Adams who visited Cincinnati to dedicate the city's original Observatory.

After walking 1 block you will come to the Ida St. bridge (1) which yields an expansive view of the lower Mill Creek Valley to the west. Completed in 1931, the current reinforced concrete bridge replaced an older wooden structure. At the north end of the bridge is the Pilgrim Presbyterian Church (2), dating from 1887.

Beyond the bridge is the Rookwood Pottery building (3). Formerly a bustling pottery works, which moved to Mt. Adams in 1892, the structure now houses an appealing restaurant and bar. Walk to the back of the parking lot between Rookwood and the Celestial Tower (4) for a spectacular view of downtown Cincinnati and the Riverfront area.

Across from the Celestial Tower is a plaque (5) that briefly describes the history of this hilltop community. Backtrack along Ida St. for ½ block and turn right on Monastery St., ascending a steep hill. Turn right along St. Paul St. for a short walk past the grounds of the Holy Cross Monastery (6). Completed in 1899, the Monastery occupies the original site of the Cincinnati Observatory. The latter was moved to its current location, in Mt. Lookout, in 1875.

Descend along Pavilion St. (see map), cross over St. Gregory St. and continue east for 1½ blocks. Turn right along the driveway that leads back to the Church of the Immaculate Conception (7). Built in 1862, this prominent Cincinnati landmark is a Good Friday pilgrimage site for Tristate Catholics. From its portico one has a sweeping view of the Ohio Valley, Northern Kentucky and the Cincinnati basin.

Descend the stairway (8) to St. Gregory St. Turn right and follow this street through the central village area. St. Gregory is the "Main St." of Mt. Adams and many of the area's most popular cafes and nightclubs are clustered near its course. One of these, Longworth's Restaurant (9), occupies an old firehouse that was built in 1887.

At the north end of St. Gregory St., turn right for ½ block and then left on Louden St. Walk 1 block and turn left, following Paradrome St. and Mt. Adams Circle back to Ida St. (see map). Cincinnati's Playhouse in the Park (10) sits on a wooded hill to your right. Opened in 1960, the Playhouse will celebrate the start of its 30th season in September, 1989. For more on the Playhouse see the Eden Park tour.

Return to your car via Ida St. Your roller coaster stroll through Mt. Adams has totalled 1.4 miles.

Shadows highlight the angular homes of Mt. Adams

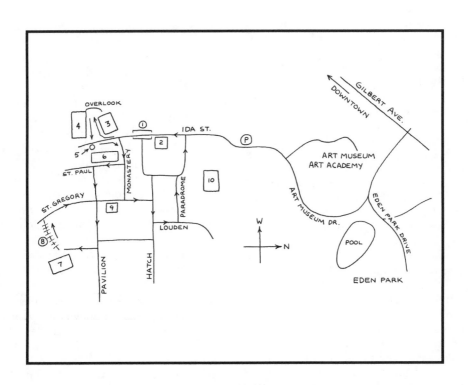

MT. ADAMS

37 STANBERY PARK

Stanbery Creek Trail
Distance: 1.5 miles
Terrain: hilly; steep areas

Stanbery Park's 31 acres sprawl across the western flank of the Mt. Washington ridge, just east of the lower Little Miami Valley. The former estate of General Sanford Stanbery and his wife, Mamie, the land was acquired by the city of Cincinnati in 1940.

The Stanbery's old, stone house (1) still stands on the property. Just east of the house is a bronze statue/fountain (2) depicting a young boy with a book. The statue, cast in Yellow Springs, Ohio, was erected in 1938 by the Civic Club of Mt. Washington.

The Park's trails are somewhat rugged, with steep areas, narrow catwalks and slippery stream crossings. The main route, known as the **Stanbery Creek Trail** (A) , is included in the National Recreation Trail system. This 1.5 mile loop winds along the primary forks of Stanbery Creek, connected to the ridgetop path by spur trails (see map).

Enter the trail just west of the parking lot, adjacent to a yellow post (3). Wind downstream through a beautiful ravine speckled with huge beech trees. Side loops lead down to the creek where small waterfalls splash over ledges of shale and limestone. Fossil hunters will find numerous bryozoans and brachiopods in these ancient, Ordovician rocks.

Just past the primary streamside loop (4), the trail narrows and clings to the edge of the cliff, crossing two small bridges. It then descends to the creek bed, crosses the stream and follows the western bank for a short distance.

Recross the creek where another trail (B) climbs to the ridgetop shelter (5). Continue downstream along the creek's eastern bank and follow the trail as it curves to the right and gently ascends along the north fork of Stanbery Creek. After crossing numerous side streams the trail emerges from the forest at the bottom of the Park's natural amphitheater (6). Climb this hillside and return to the lot, completing a 1.5 mile loop.

As is evident from the map, one can lengthen or shorten the hike by choosing alternative routes. The "B" trail, descending from the shelter to Stanbery Creek, is relatively gentle and footing is good. However, the "C" trail is precipitous and should be avoided by most hikers.

To reach Stanbery Park from downtown Cincinnati, follow Columbia Parkway (U.S 50) east for approximately 4.5 miles. Turn right on Stanley Ave., drive 2 blocks and turn left on Kellogg Ave. (U.S 52). Drive 2.3 miles and bear right onto Salem Pike, which circles back across Kellogg Ave. and winds up the Mt. Washington ridge. Follow this road for 2.1 miles and turn left on Sutton Rd. Drive 1.4 miles, curve to the right for 1 block and turn left on Oxford Ave. The Park entrance will be ½ block on your left.

Scene along Stanbery Creek

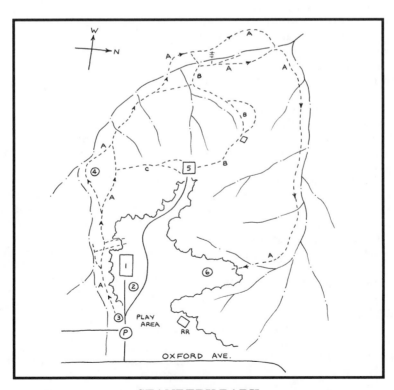

STANBERY PARK

38 LUNKEN AIRPORT

Hike Bike Trail
Distance: 6.2 miles
Terrain: flat

When Lunken Airport was dedicated, in 1932, it was the largest municipal airport in the United States. However, in the decades following the opening of the Boone County Airport (now Greater Cincinnati International Airport), Lunken, the original home of American Airlines, reverted to a set of sleepy runways in the lowlands of eastern Hamilton County. Visitors would stop by to watch an occasional piper cub drift in along the Little Miami Valley.

With increasing traffic at Greater Cincinnati International, growing interest in private aviation, improved flood control and the arrival of the corporate jet age, Lunken Airport has experienced a renewal in the 1980's. This resurgence of aviation has been matched by an influx of joggers, walkers and cyclists to the Airport's flatlands.

A 6.2 mile **Hike/Bike Trail** loops around the airfield. Access to the trail is provided by parking areas along Airport Rd. or at the playground, north of Lunken (see map). The western rim of the loop parallels Wilmer Ave. while its eastern and southern sections run atop flood control levees. These elevated pathways offer broad views of the Airport and surrounding hills. In addition, the levees are flanked by thickets and woodlands, providing an excellent avenue for birdwatching. Indeed, veteran birders flock to Lunken each winter to look for short-eared owls, which arrive from Canada to hunt on the valley's grasslands.

Of historical interest is Pioneer Cemetery, located along Wilmer Ave., 1 block north of Airport Rd. (see map). This small plot contains the graves of Major Benjamin Stites and the other New Jersey citizens who founded the settlement of Columbia here in November, 1788. Their town pre-dated Losantiville (Cincinnati) by 1 month.

Attracted to the area by the fertile "Turkey Bottoms" of the Little Miami floodplain, the settlers clustered their log homes near a stockade for protection from regional Indians. They erected the Northwest Territory's first Protestant church, in 1790.

The ornate column (1) at the top of the cemetery steps honors "The first boat load" of settlers who now lie beneath weathered limestone markers. Major Benjamin Stites' gravestone (2) was replaced in November, 1923, at a ceremony commemorating the 135th anniversary of Columbia's founding.

To reach Lunken Airport from downtown Cincinnati, follow Columbia Parkway (U.S. 50 east) for approximately 4.5 miles. Turn right on Stanley Ave., drive two blocks and turn left on Kellogg Ave. (U.S. 52). Drive approximately 1 mile and turn left on Wilmer Ave. Park along Airport Rd. or at the playground, north of Lunken (see map).

If possible, plan a weekday visit to avoid the weekend crush of joggers and cyclists. In addition, due to the open, flat terrain and funneling effect of adjacent ridges, be advised that the wind-chill factor can be severe during the colder months.

Summer along the Hike/Bike Trail

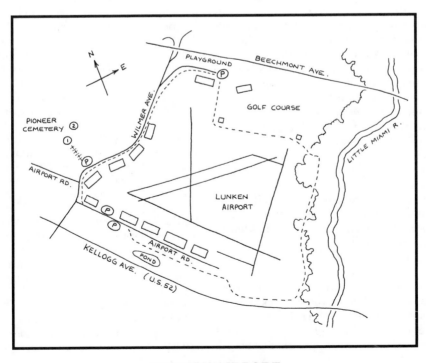

LUNKEN AIRPORT

39 DEVOU PARK

Nature Trail
  Distance: 1.25 miles
  Terrain: hilly; steep areas

Overlook Hike
  Distance: 2.2 miles
  Terrain: rolling

To many Cincinnatians, Devou Park, in Northern Kentucky, is known for two things. First, it harbors a spectacular view of Covington and the Cincinnati basin. Second, it's hard to find.

To deal with the latter problem first, follow I-75 south into Kentucky and take the Ky. 1072/Ft. Wright Exit (Exit #189-B). Bear right off the exit and turn right onto Dixie Highway. Drive 1 block and turn left on Sleepy Hollow Rd. (Ky. 1072). Bear left and wind downhill. Drive 1.7 miles to the Park's entrance, on your right (just before the railroad trestle).

Follow Devou Park Rd. until it deadends into Montague (see map). Turn right and then bear right into the golf course/tennis area. Park in the lot adjacent to the clubhouse (1).

Devou Park's 550 ridgetop acres were donated to the city of Covington in 1910. For an overview of the Park, we suggest the following two hikes.

Nature Trail. Devou Park's 1.25 mile Nature Trail originates along the gravel service road that crosses between the golf course (2) and the tennis complex (3). Hike westward along the road until it turns sharply to the left. Find the trail to the right of this bend (see map) and descend into the ravine via a series of switchbacks and stairways.

Near the bottom, the trail loops to the left, following a small creek, and then turns upstream along the primary channel. Angling to the left, ascend the hillside, crossing the service road, and wind through the ridgetop forest. Turn right at the trail intersection, as

illustrated on the map. The trail eventually emerges from the woodland near the tennis courts.

The Sierra Club of Northern Kentucky has directed efforts to improve Devou Park's Nature Trail.

Overlook Hike. Unfortunately, except for the Nature Trail, Devou Park does not currently provide hike/bike paths for exercise conscious visitors. The following walk to Lookout Point (4), from the clubhouse area, (1), thus parallels the Park's roadways, crossing open lawns along the way.

Walk northward on Montague and turn right at the first intersection (see map), passing the Park's natural amphitheater (5). Bear right and wind downhill along West Park Rd. Turn left at the intersection, climbing the ridge, and bear right into the Lookout area. From the overlook the visitor enjoys an expansive view of Covington, the Ohio Valley and the Cincinnati basin, flanked by ridgetop neighborhoods.

Return along Park Lane which merges with Jerol Ave. Be sure to stop at the Behringer-Crawford Museum (6) which houses a collection of artifacts, maps and exhibits, depicting the natural history and early industries of Northern Kentucky. The Museum is open Tuesday through Saturday, 10 am to 5 pm and Sunday, 1 pm to 5 pm. It is closed on Mondays, most holidays and during the month of January. Admission fee is currently $1.00 for adults and $.50 for children

Follow Montague Rd. back to the clubhouse area, completing a loop of 2.2 miles.

The Cincinnati basin from Devou's overlook

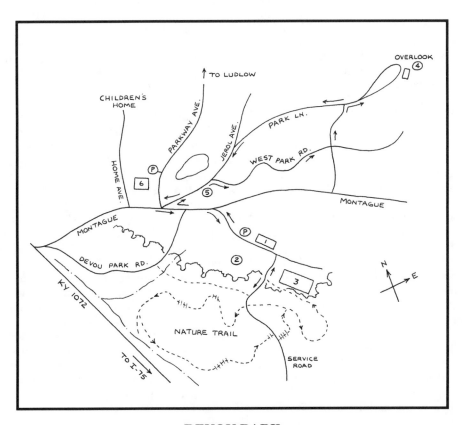

DEVOU PARK

Distance: 2.7 miles
Terrain: flat

The original settlement of Covington, Kentucky, nestled in the west Licking Valley, was platted in 1815. The town was bounded by 6th and Washington Sts. and by the Ohio and Licking Rivers. Incorporated as a city in 1835, Covington expanded to the south and west.

The West Side District was the second major addition to the city's original layout. Bordered to the west by Willow Run Creek, this neighborhood was sparsely settled until the influx of German immigrants in the 1840's. Much of the District's land had been owned by James Riddle, who operated a farm, mill, distillery and ferry service from his west Covington property. When the Bank of the United States foreclosed on Riddle's estate in 1830, the land was opened up for residential settlement.

The German immigrants built closely spaced "rowhouses" which still typify the area today. In an effort to preserve these structures and to draw tourists to this historic district, the MainStrasse Village Association was formed in 1978. With the aid of a $2.5 million grant from Kentucky's Board of Tourism, many homes and commercial buildings have been restored. The core of this redevelopment is centered around the intersection of 6th and Main Streets, where shops have clustered along the open mall. Covington's West Side District was added to the National Register of Historic Places in 1982.

For a walking tour of the District, park along Philadelphia St. which borders Goebel Park (1). The Park's clock tower (2), constructed in the late 1970's reflects the German heritage of the neighborhood. Walk east along 6th St. The dome and steeples of the Mother of God Church (4) loom in the distance. The 6th St. Mall, site of Covington's annual Oktoberfest, is lined with shops that retain the flavor of the mid 1800's. A fountain (3), depicting a girl carrying two geese, graces the corner of 6th and Main.

Continue east on 6th St., pass under the railroad bridge, bearing right and then left. The Mother of God Church (4), at 6th and Washington, was built in 1871. Organized in 1841 by Rev. Ferdinand Kuhr, this is the second oldest parish in Covington. The Church's dome was destroyed by fire on September 25, 1986, but was rebuilt within a year. Its twin steeples rise 200 ft. above the city and the building's interior is adorned with stained glass, frescoes and murals of German origin. Across 6th St. from the Church, Tickets, (5), a new restaurant and nightclub, occupies an old firehouse, dating from the mid 1800's

Continue east for 1 block and turn right (south) along Madison Ave., Covington's true "Main St." Walk ½ block and turn right, cutting through a plaza (6), lined with shops. This mall leads into 7th/Pike Streets. (see map). Continue west for 1 block and turn left along Russell St.

Russell St. is lined with refurbished, closely-spaced homes which typify this historic area. The Sandford House (7), in the 1000 block, dates from the early 1800's. Built on land originally owned by General Thomas Sandford, Northern Kentucky's first Congressman, the house was purchased by the Western Baptist Theologic Institute in 1835. The Institute closed in 1853 due to dissension over the slavery issue.

Turn left (east) on 11th St., cross the bridge and descend to Madison Ave. The Cathedral Basilica of the Assumption (8), dedicated in 1901, fills most of the block to the southeast. Its facade is modeled after the Notre Dame Cathedral, in Paris. Three frescoes by Frank Duveneck, Covington's native son and a former Dean at Cincinnati's Art Academy, adorn the Church's interior.

MainStrasse Village

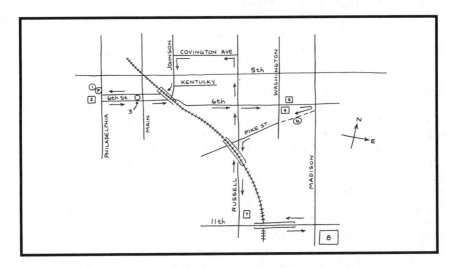

WEST COVINGTON/MAINSTRASSE

Retrace your route along 11th and Russell Sts. Continue north on Russell, crossing over 6th and 5th Sts. Turn left along Covington Ave., a cobblestone alley lined with attractive, 19th Century rowhouses.

Turn left (south) on Johnson St. Kentucky Ave., on your left between 5th and 6th Sts., is another block of fine, refurbished rowhouses. Turn right on 6th St. and return to Goebel Park. Your walking tour of West Covington/MainStrasse has totalled 2.7 miles

To reach MainStrasse Village from Cincinnati, cross the Suspension Bridge and follow Court Ave. to 4th St. Turn right (west), drive 6½ blocks and turn left on Philadelphia St., which borders Goebel Park (see map). Alternatively, follow I-75 to the Covington/Ludlow Exit (Exit #192), turn east on 5th St. and then right on Philadelphia.

41 COVINGTON RIVERSIDE DISTRICT AND SUSPENSION BRIDGE

Distance: 2.5 miles
Terrain: mostly flat; few stairways

A walk through Covington's Riverside Drive Historic Area is easily combined with a stroll across Greater Cincinnati's most famous bridge. Park in one of the lots along Pete Rose Way, just west of Riverfront Stadium (1). Cross the road and ascend the stairs to the bridge's entry ramp (see map).

The John A Roebling Suspension Bridge (2) opened to traffic on New Year's Day, 1867, after ten years of construction. Its architect, John Roebling, used this experience in his later design of New York's Brooklyn Bridge. The Suspension Bridge stretches 2252 feet across the Ohio and is the oldest bridge that still spans the River today.

At the south end of the bridge, turn left along E. 2nd St. for ½ block and then left on Greenup St. The Riverside Plaza Condominiums (3), at E. 2nd and Greenup, are part of Covington's Riverside Development Project. The complex consists of two buildings, Riverside Terrace, completed in 1984, and Riverside Plaza, which opened in 1986. Combined, the buildings contain 85 units, including modern townhouses designed to blend with the nearby Shinkle Row (15). Many of the units open onto terraced decks, overlooking the Ohio River.

North of the Condominium complex is a bronze statue of John A. Roebling (4), architect of the Suspension Bridge. It is one of seven statues that are spaced along Covington's Riverside Walk, depicting individuals who played important roles in the city's development. The bronze statues were dedicated in October, 1988.

Walk east along Riverside Drive which is lined with large, ante-bellum houses. Strolling down this majestic avenue, one is reminded of southern port cities such as Charleston and Savannah. On the southeast corner of Garrard St. and Riverside Drive is George Rogers Clark Park, adorned with statues of Simon Kenton (5) and Captain Mary B. Greene (6). Simon Kenton, one of the first men to explore and settle the Covington area, is the person for whom Kenton County was named. Captain Greene was one of the few women to command a riverboat, playing an important role in the city's early economy.

Further east along Riverside Drive, James Bradley (7) relaxes on a bench. An eloquent abolitionist and former slave, Mr. Bradley took part in the famous Lane Seminary debates.

At the junction of Riverside Drive and Shelby St. are two more figures. Chief Little Turtle (8), leader of the Miami Indian tribe, points across the Ohio while John James Audubon (9), the renowned naturalist and artist, faces the mouth of the Licking River.

Angle south along Shelby St., passing a cluster of new townhomes. Turn right on E. 2nd St. The Mimosa House Museum (10), built in 1853, is an original Italianate structure that underwent Colonial-Revival restoration in 1900. Daniel Fallis, a prominent Cincinnati banker, and his descendents occupied the house from 1861 to 1950. Today, the building is operated as a house museum by a nonprofit organization. Tours of the house are conducted on weekends, from 1 to 6 pm; a fee of $3.00 per person is requested.

The Lowry-Laidley House (11), at 404 E. 2nd St., was constructed about 1870. It offers an example of Italianate architecture, complete with mansard roof and Victorian Gothic moldings.

The Carneal House (12), more properly called the Gano-Southgate House, sits above the southeast corner of Kennedy and E. 2nd St. Built in 1815, it is the oldest brick house in Covington and is thought to have been built for John S. Gano, the city's founder. A tunnel, used to hide runaway slaves, leads from its basement to the west bank of the Licking

James Bradley Statue

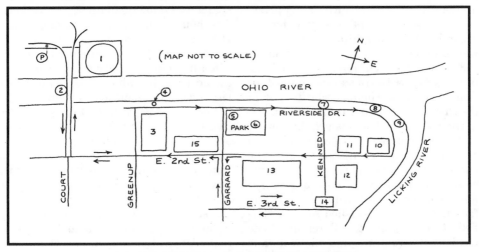

COVINGTON RIVERSIDE DISTRICT

River.

Continuing west on E. 2nd St. you will pass the Governors Point Condominiums (13) which occupy the former site and structure of Wm. Booth Memorial Hospital. The central, 5-story building dates from the mid 1920s.

Turn left (south) on Garrard St. and then left on E. 3rd St. The former home of Daniel Carter Beard (14), first National Commissioner of the Boy Scouts of America, sits at the east end of the block. This 1820 Victorian home has been designated a National Historic Landmark. Beard, whose statue graces the home, founded the "Sons of Daniel Boone" which became the Boy Scouts of America in 1910.

Backtrack along Third and Garrard Streets and turn left along E. 2nd. The Shinkle Row Houses (15) were officially recognized by the Miami Purchase Association in 1976, honoring their attractive and detailed restoration.

Continue west on E. 2nd St. and then re-cross the Suspension Bridge. Your scenic and historic tour has totalled 2.5 miles. For more information on this interesting area, contact the Licking Riverside Civic Association.

42 FORT THOMAS MILITARY RESERVATION/TOWER PARK

Distance: 1.4 miles
Terrain: flat

Ft. Thomas, Kentucky, sits 300 feet above the Ohio River Valley. Incorporated in 1914, the city formed around a Federal military outpost that was established on this high ridge in 1887. The Fort itself, replacing the flood-prone Newport Barracks, was named for General George Thomas who fought in the Civil, Mexican and Indian Wars.

The city of Ft. Thomas acquired much of the Reservation in December, 1972, and established "Tower Park" on the site. The latter now includes playgrounds, tennis courts, a baseball field, a natural amphitheater and indoor athletic facilities at the refurbished Armory. The Federal Government still retains some residential structures and the Veterans Administration Nursing Home on the Reservation grounds.

A walk through this 111 acre preserve offers a pleasing blend of history and natural scenery. Park in one of the lots at the Douglas St. entrance (see map). A 90-foot, limestone tower, constructed in 1898, stands near the entrance and commemorates soldiers of the 6th Regiment of the U.S. Infantry who fought in the Spanish American War.

Walk east along Cochran, past the Park's amphitheater (see map). This drive leads out to Alexander Circle where a cluster of brick homes enjoy a spectacular view of the Ohio River Valley. The view extends from Lunken Airport to the north and follows the River south, past Old Coney, Riverbend and River Downs. The Cincinnati Waterworks can be seen across from the Fort and the I-275 bridge spans the Ohio just south of the overlook. The houses on the Circle belong to the U.S. Government and are used by employees of the V.A. Nursing Home.

Return along the drive that passes to the north of the ball field (see map). Turn left and follow Cochran Ave. south. Green St., on your right, is lined with the former homes of military personnel, now occupied by Ft. Thomas residents. Continue along Cochran, passing the Veterans Administration Nursing Home. This building, completed in 1934, was initially used as a military barrack. It served briefly as an Air Force hospital in the 1950's before it became the Tristate region's V.A. Nursing Home in the mid 1960's.

Turn right along Carmel Manor Drive and cut through the small parking area that serves a group of shops on S. Ft. Thomas Ave. Turn right and follow this main route northward, paralleling the western edge of the Reservation. The old Armory, now a component of Tower Park, houses basketball courts, a game room and community exercise facilities. Returning to the Park's entrance, your walking tour has totalled 1.4. miles.

To reach Tower Park and the Ft. Thomas Military Reservation, take I-471 to the Grand Ave./Ky 1892 Exit (Exit #3). Turn east and follow Grand Ave. as it winds up the ridge. Drive 1.7 miles and turn right on S. Ft. Thomas Ave. Proceed 2 blocks to the Park entrance, on your left.

Alexander Circle hugs the edge of the Ft. Thomas ridge.

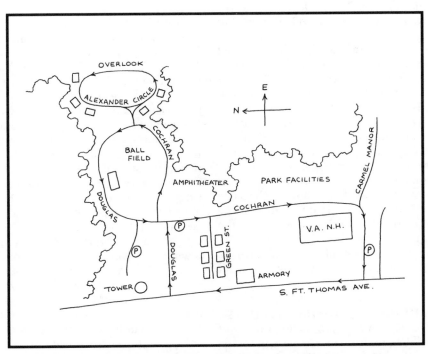

TOWER PARK/FT. THOMAS MILITARY RESERVATION

43 CALIFORNIA WOODS NATURE PRESERVE

California Junction Trail
  Distance: 1.25 miles
  Terrain: hilly; few steep areas

Combined Trail
  Distance: 2.0 miles
  Terrain: hilly; steep sections

California Woods Nature Preserve is draped over two parallel ridges near the mouth of the Little Miami River. Established in 1937 and managed by the Cincinnati Recreation Commission, the Preserve's 110 acres are cloaked with a mature maple-beech forest. Huge sycamores rise along the creek beds and tulip trees speckle the woodland. Forest wildflowers are abundant in spring and birdwatching is excellent here throughout the year.

A network of eleven trails provides access to the Preserve. Two of these, the California Junction Trail (1) and the Trillium Valley Trail (2), have received designation as National Recreation Trails.

To reach California Woods from downtown Cincinnati, follow U.S. 50 (Columbia Parkway) east for approximately 4.5 miles. Turn right on Stanley Ave., drive 2 blocks and turn left on Kellogg Ave. (U.S. 52). Continue eastward for approximately 2.3 miles, crossing the Little Miami River. The Preserve's entrance will be on your left, approximately .5 mile east of the River. Park in the gravel lot along the left side of the entry road (see map). A small usage fee is charged to fund maintenance of the refuge.

For an overview of California Woods we recommend the following two trail loops:

California Junction Trail (1). Dedicated as a National Recreation Trail in October, 1988, this 1.25 mile loop begins along the entry road, approximately 50 yards south of the parking lot (see map). It first skirts a creek bed and then ascends the ridge via a series of earthen steps. At the top of the hill, turn right along a straight, level section of the trail. You are following the old bed of the Cincinnati-Georgetown & Portsmouth Railroad. Opened in 1878, the rail line shut down during the great 1937 flood. California Woods was the "junction" where a side track angled off to Coney Island.

At the north end of the loop the trail passes through a shelter house, veers to the left and descends onto the Little Miami floodplain. Paralleling Kellogg Ave., the trail crosses several small streams and gradually ascends the southern flank of the ridge. It soon rejoins the old railroad bed, clearly demarcated by the levee-like topography. The visitor will notice the disrupted drainage pattern that resulted from the bed's construction. Completing the loop, descend via the entry trail.

Combined Loop Trail. Begin this 2.0 mile route at the Trillium Valley Trailhead, just south of the parking lot. The Trillium Valley Trail (2) is named for the abundant white trillium that covers this area in the spring. Climb along the south edge of a deep ravine and follow the trail as it curves to the right, crossing the primary stream. The trail continues higher along a tributary channel before turning eastward and dipping through a shallow ravine. Wind along the top of the ridge via the Moon Ridge Trail (3), bearing left at the intersections with the Ravine (4) and Beech (5) Trails.

Descend along Twin Oaks Trail (6) toward the Nature Center building (7). Angle left onto the Lower Thicket Trail (8), crossing several small streams (see map). At the northern end of the loop the trail descends to the creek basin. Cross Lick Run via a series of large rocks and cut through the streamside woodland to the Preserve's central roadway.

Autumn in the Lick Run Valley

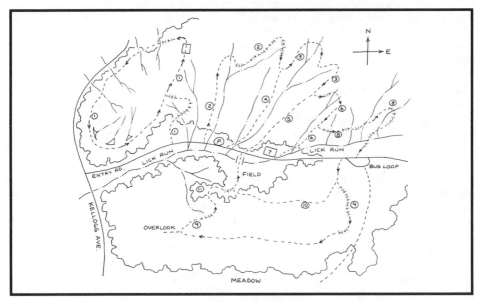

CALIFORNIA WOODS

Turn right along the road, walk 50 yards and pick up the entry trail to the Upper (9) and Lower (10) Ridge Trails, just south of the bus loop (see map). Ascend the earthen stairs and bear left along the Upper Ridge Trail (9). This high ground separates the Lick Run Valley from a broad meadow to the east. Hike southward along the crest of the ridge which yields expansive views in the winter. A faint spur trail leads to an overlook at the south end of the loop.

The trail descends into the valley via broad switchbacks. Near the bottom of the slope a "natural classroom" (11) occupies a clearing to the left of the trail. Cross the field to the bridge and then return to your car along the roadway.

44 WITHROW NATURE PRESERVE

Trout Lily Trail
   Distance: 2.0 miles
   Terrain: Old Farm loop: rolling
         Hepatica Hill loop: steep hills

Thanks to the generosity of Eugene and Adelaide Farny and through the efforts of the Ohio Nature Conservancy, Cincinnatians have a beautiful 273 acre refuge in eastern Hamilton County. Withrow Nature Preserve, added to the Park District lands in October, 1983, is well known for its great variety of wildflowers. A visit in spring or early summer is highly recommended.

To reach the Preserve, follow I-275 to the eastern side of Hamilton County. Take the Five Mile Rd. Exit (Exit #69) and head south, toward the Ohio River. The entrance to the Preserve will be on your left.

Trout Lily Trail. Withrow Nature Preserve's two-mile Trout Lily Trail is divided into two loops. Enter at the trailhead, just south of the parking area (see map). After walking a short distance the trail diverges toward the Old Farm Loop (left) and the Hepatica Hill Loop (right). Bear left onto the Old Farm loop (A). This 1.75 mile route first winds through a mature forest, crossing small streams along the way. Gentle hills are encountered but the trail is well maintained and footing is good.

At the fork in the trail (see map) angle to the right and head toward the overlook. A spur trail leads out to this clearing at the edge of the ridge, yielding a broad view of the Ohio Valley. During the warmer months, turkey vultures soar above the ridge, catching updrafts along the valley wall.

The main trail continues through mixed woodland, joins a gravel road bed and passes an old cabin. It then returns to the entry trail, crossing open fields. White-tailed deer often browse in these meadows at dawn or dusk. In addition, a twilight visit may turn up a great horned owl as it emerges from the forest to hunt on the fields. Other residents include raccoons, woodchucks and pileated woodpeckers.

Upon reaching the entry trail, bear left along the Hepatica Hill loop (B). This .25 mile dip through the forest crosses an area where wildflowers abound during the spring and early summer. A brochure, provided by the Park District, illustrates some of the plants that can be found along the trail. These include trout lilies, hepatica, shooting star, trillium, Dutchman's breeches, squirrel corn, bloodroot, bluebells and Christmas ferns.

Winding into the forest, the Hepatica loop angles to the left and descends along a stairway. It then turns westward and roller-coasters through the woodland before climbing the ridge via a series of stairs and decks. Emerging behind the Highwood Lodge, turn left and walk back to the parking area.

Scene along the Old Farm Loop

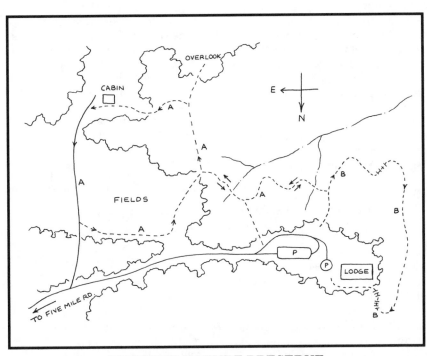

WITHROW NATURE PRESERVE

45 WOODLAND MOUND PARK

Combined Trail Route
Distance: 1.8 miles
Terrain: hilly; steep areas

Cincinnati's numerous hills and ridges are heavily wooded. Extensive views are obtained only where roads or parks hug the edge of a cliff.

Woodland Mound Park, near the eastern end of Hamilton County, is an exception to that rule. Sprawling across a ridgetop, the Park's central corridor has been cleared of trees. Forest cloaks the hillsides but grasslands, ball fields and playgrounds give the area an unusual openness along the Ohio Valley. Though far less spectacular, one is reminded of the southern Appalachian "balds" or western alpine meadows when hiking across the ridge.

A site for the Park was first targeted in the 1930's. After many years of land acquisition, Woodland Mound Park was finally dedicated in July, 1980. It now sprawls across 900 acres. The constant breeze affords a cool retreat in summer and attracts kite flyers throughout the warmer months.

To reach the Park, follow I-275 to eastern Hamilton County. Take the Beechmont Ave./Ohio Route 125 Exit (Exit #65). Proceed west on Beechmont Ave. for approximately .9 mile to Nordyke Rd. This intersection is controlled by a stoplight and a Volvo dealership is on its southeast corner. Turn left on Nordyke and drive approximately 2 miles to the Park entrance, on your right. Daily usage fee is $1.00 per vehicle; an annual pass to all Hamilton County Parks can be obtained for $3.00.

Park in the lot at the eastern end of the ridge which serves the Weston Amphitheater (1). The latter, named for Sarah Weston, seats 10,000 on a sloping lawn and is the site for various concerts, including appearances by the Cincinnati Symphony Orchestra, during the summer months.

Our 1.8 mile hike combines a short walk out to the Amphitheater overlook, a hike along the Hedgeapple Nature Trail (A) and a stroll through the Park's Parcours route (B). Walk out to the Amphitheater stage for a spectacular view of the Ohio Valley. Except for distant power plants, the view is remarkably free of modern structures.

Backtrack toward the parking lot and angle onto the Hedgeapple Trail (A). Named for the hedgeapple (osage orange) trees that are common here, this .6 mile loop dips through the forest, following a figure-eight route (see map). The terrain is steep and footing is uneven in some areas. A brochure, available at the Breezy Point Pavilion (2), illustrates natural highlights along the trail. Near the bottom of the loop, a frog pond provides entertainment for children and a reststop for adults during the warmer months.

Completing the Nature Trail loop, turn right and pick up Woodland Mound's 1-mile Parcours Trail (B). Follow this wide, gentle path as its skirts an open meadow and descends into a shallow ravine. Bear right at the trail intersection, cross the creek and ascend a short stairway. Turn right, paralleling the stream along a level, hillside path. Follow the trail to the left and circle a clearing where stone steps, a rock wall and other artifacts reveal the site of an abandoned homestead. After a respite at this pleasant spot, retrace your route to the parking area.

View from The Hedgeapple Trail

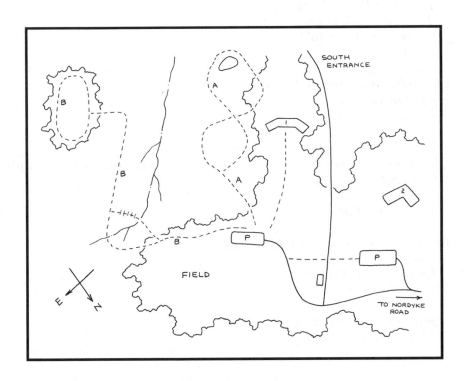

WOODLAND MOUND'S TRAILS

Appendix

Local Conservation/
Preservation Organizations

Audubon Society of Ohio
2073 Harrison Ave.
Cincinnati, Ohio 45214
481-0305

Cincinnati Historical Society
Eden Park
Cincinnati, Ohio 45202
241-4622

Cincinnati Nature Center
4949 Tealtown Rd.
Milford, Ohio 45150
831-1711

Cincinnati Park Board
950 Eden Park Drive
Cincinnati, Ohio 45202
352-4080

Cincinnati Recreation Commission
644 Linn St.
Cincinnati, Ohio 45203
352-4000

**Cincinnati Wildflower Preservation Society/Southwest Chapter,
Ohio Native Plant Society**
338 Compton Rd.
Wyoming, Ohio 45215

Friends of Cincinnati Parks, Inc.
950 Eden Park Drive
Cincinnati, Ohio 45202
352-4080

Glendale Heritage Preservation
Glendale, Ohio 45246

Hamilton County Park District
10245 Winton Rd.
Cincinnati, Ohio 45231
East District Naturalist: 563-4513
West District Naturalist: 385-4811

Hillside Trust
3012 Section Rd., at French Park
Cincinnati, Ohio 45237
531-6334

Historic Conservation Office
Cincinnati Planning Department
Room 228, City Hall
801 Plum St.
Cincinnati, Ohio 45202
352-3478

Historic Preservation Office
Economic Development Department
18 Pike St.
Covington, Kentucky 41011
292-2111

Little Miami, Inc.
3012 Section Rd., at French Park
Cincinnati, Ohio 45237
351-6400

MainStrasse Village Association
616 Main St.
Covington, Kentucky 41011
491-0458

Miami Purchase Association
Hamilton County Memorial Building
1225 Elm St.
Cincinnati, Ohio 45210
721-4506

Milford Historical Society
Promont
906 Main St.
Milford, Ohio 45150
248-0324

Montgomery Historical Society
7650 Cooper Rd.
Montgomery, Ohio 45242
891-2421

National Register of Historic Places
National Park Service
U.S. Department of the Interior
Washington, D.C. 20240

The Nature Conservancy
Ohio Field Office
1504 W. First Ave.
Columbus, Ohio 43212-3495
614-486-4194

Ohio Department of Natural Resources
Division of Natural Areas & Preserves
1889 Fountain Square
Columbus, Ohio 43224

Oxbow, Inc.
2073 Harrison Ave.
Cincinnati, Ohio 45214

RAPTOR, Inc.
2073 Harrison Ave.
Cincinnati, Ohio 45214

Rivers Unlimited
3012 Section Rd., at French Park
Cincinnati, Ohio 45237
351-4417

Sierra Club
6425 Orchard Ln.
Cincinnati, Ohio
841-0111

Wyoming Historical Preservation Commission
Wyoming, Ohio
761-3259

Bibliography

1. Arcilesi, Leonard, "A Historical Sketch of Hughes High School," Cincinnati, Ohio

2. Beasley, David, "Happy Birthday MainStrasse!" Tristate Magazine, Cincinnati Enquirer, 9/4/88

3. Bicentennial Flashback Series, The Cincinnati Enquirer, 1988

4. "The Bicentennial Riverwalk," Greater Cincinnati Bicentennial Commission, 1988

5. Brady, Lilia, "A Walk Through History," Cincinnati Magazine, May, 1988

6. "Brief History of Memorial Hall," The Miami Purchase Association, Cincinnati, Ohio, June, 1988

7. Caldwell Park Trail Map, Cincinnati Park Board

8. California Woods Nature Preserve Trail Map, Cincinnati Recreation Commission

9. **Cincinnati, A Guide to the Queen City and Its Neighborhoods,** Writers' Program, Ohio, American Guide Series, 1943, sponsored by City of Cincinnati

10. "Cincinnati Centerpiece," Progressive Architecture, October, 1985

11. Cincinnati Nature Center Trail Map, Cincinnati Nature Center, Milford, Ohio

12. DeBosse, Jim, "Landmarks: 2088, What Should Our City Save for the Future?" Cincinnati Enquirer, 10/21/88

13. "The Early History of Clifton, (from Nellie Brown's Scrapbook)" courtesy Miami Purchase Association

14. Evergreen Magazine, Hamilton County Park District, Jim Rahtz, Editor, Cincinnati, Ohio

15. "Exhibit: A Tour of Cincinnati Firehouse History," Datebook, Cincinnati Enquirer, Mary Napier, Editor, 12/18/88

16. Feck, Luke, **Yesterday's Cincinnati,** Writers' Digest Books, F&W Publications, Inc., Cincinnati, 1975, 1987

17. **Glendale's Heritage,** Glendale Heritage Preservation, Glendale, Ohio, 1976

18. Green, Richard, "Landmark Getting Facelift, Doctors Building to be Presidential Plaza," Cincinnati Enquirer, November 27, 1988

19. Hamilton County Park District Nature Trail Guides, 10245 Winton Rd., Cincinnati, Ohio 45231

20. Harmon, Frances, "History Quiz" (Old Woodward High Building), Tristate Magazine, Cincinnati Enquirer, 8/21/88

21. "Historic Walking Tour, Wyoming, Ohio," Wyoming Historical Preservation Commission, April, 1988

22. Hume, Paul, "Cincinnati: New Music Complex, U.S. Premiere," Washington Post, 4/15/72 (entered into Congressional Record of 4/18/72)

23. Kayser, Pat, **Cincinnati Without Fears or Tears, Indispensable Guide to Cincinnati,** Bicentennial Edition, Pat Kayser Books, Inc., Cincinnati, 1988

24. "Landmarks of Historic Montgomery, A Walking Tour," Montgomery Landmarks Commission, Montgomery, Ohio, October, 1983

25. Langsam, Walter C. and Julianne Warren, **Cincinnati in Color,** Hastings House Publishers, New York, 1978

26. Linden-Ward, Blanche, "Spring Grove Cemetery, A Self-Guided Walking Tour," Center of Neighborhood and Community Studies, University of Cincinnati, 1985

27. "Little Miami Scenic River Basin Trail," Loveland Chamber of Commerce, Loveland, Ohio

28. "The Little Miami State and National Scenic River," Ohio's Scenic Rivers, Division of Natural Areas and Preserves, Ohio Department of Natural Resources, Columbus, Ohio

29. Maslowski, Karl, "An Old Path Becomes a New Trail," Naturalist Afield, Tristate Magazine, Cincinnati Enquirer, 10/30/88

30. "Milford, Ohio. A Walking Tour of Old Miford" The Milford Historical Society

31. "Milford. A Pleasant Blend of Tradition & Progress" Milford Area Chamber of Commerce

32. Mt. Airy Forest Map, Board of Park Commissioners, City of Cincinnati, revised 6/4/81

33. National Register of Historic Places, National Park Service, U.S. Department of Interior, Washington, D.C.

34. **Ohio Almanac 1970,** The Lorain Journal Company, Lorain, Ohio

35. "The Renton K. Brodie Science & Engineering Complex," The Flow Sheet, Department of Chemical & Metallurgical Engineering, University of Cincinnati, February, 1968

36. Steinfirst, Donald, "Cincinnati Opens New Concert Auditorium," Pittsburgh Post-Gazette, 12/4/67

37. Sweeney, Bobbie, "What makes Ridge so pleasant?" Suburban Life, January 7, 1976

38. "Walking Tour of the Licking Riverside Historic District," Licking Riverside Civic Association, Covington, Kentucky

39. Wetenkanmp, Elmer, "Bicentennial Commons Guide," Cincinnati Enquirer, Tempo Section, 6/2/88

40. Xavier University Admissions Manual, Xavier University, Cincinnati, Ohio, 1988

Index

114